THE HAMLYN
BASIC GUIDE TO
MACHINE
KNITTING

THE HAMLYN BASIC GUIDE TO

MACHINE KNITTING

Patricia Graham

HAMLYN

Front cover: The knitted woven jacket (pp. 96–100) and the bouclé slash neck jumper (pp. 52–6) are a stylish combination (*The Hamlyn Publishing Group/Fiona Pragoff*).
Back cover: Alternative stitch pattern (p. 93) for the V neck Fair Isle slipover, knitted in four colours (*The Hamlyn Publishing Group/David Johnson*).
Frontispiece: This colourful V neck Fair Isle (p. 93) will brighten any day (*The Hamlyn Publishing Group/Fiona Pragoff*).
Page 14–15: A Knitmaster Zippy de lux knitting machine (*The Hamlyn Publishing Group/David Johnson*).

This edition published in 1989 by
The Hamlyn Publishing Group Limited,
a division of the Octopus Publishing Group,
Michelin House, 81 Fulham Road, London SW3 6RB

ISBN 0 600 56828 8

Produced by Mandarin Offset
Printed and Bound in Hong Kong

CONTENTS

INTRODUCTION

So you want to learn how to machine knit? The idea is irresistible – lots of exciting and colourful sweaters easily knitted for you and your family, or perhaps to sell. You may already have a knitting machine (and left it under the bed), or are about to buy one, and want to learn how to achieve a never-ending variety of knitted garments flowing from your machine. If so, this is the book for you.

Machine knitting is a creative and stimulating craft open to anyone. The advantages are that the more boring parts are knitted quickly, and that you can – almost without knowing it – start to create your own designs.

In this book my aim, based on my experience teaching machine knitting to women and men of all ages, is to give the knitter sound, basic knowledge, emphasising the importance of learning how to use the machine, the common terms, and the basic techniques and skills which are essential to successful machine knitting.

HOW TO USE THIS BOOK

This book has been arranged logically, so the knitter starts at the beginning, thoroughly learning and practising those basic techniques and skills. This quickly leads on to knitting the first garment – a simple snood – and then to the slash neck jumper. With each new garment new features are introduced. The third garment, for example, introduces a round neck, set-in sleeves and slipstitch patterning.

You gradually increase your understanding of your machine and of techniques as you knit through the patterns. Several methods for each technique are given with practice instructions for you to try before you knit each garment.

Designing and knitting your own garments is not difficult. Information on how to do it is included, along with measuring instructions and measurement charts. If you have not done this before, start by adapting a known pattern – in this book the slash neck is changed to a roundneck. Knitting your own garment is very rewarding.

Opposite: *The author knitting on a Brother Electronic single bed machine.*

After you have knitted your way through all the garments, you can go back to the beginning and use the pattern features in this book over and over again in different combinations from the ones I have given – there are dozens of them. The slash-neck jumper, for example, you can make in tuck stitch, slip stitch, Fair Isle or with a single motif, and can also choose from an immense variety of yarns in wool, acrylic or cotton and an unlimited choice of tempting colours. Remember to always knit a tension swatch first when you are trying something different.

POINTERS FOR YOU

☐ No two machines will knit exactly the same way. Get to know your own machine and how it will respond.

☐ While you are learning, you can knit your early garments on cheaper acrylic yarn.

☐ If you go wrong, don't be afraid to take the knitting off the machine, rewind the yarn and start again. Knitting can be re-done quickly on a machine.

☐ Machine knitting has its own language, and in addition the manufacturers introduce their own terms.

Here, common terms are used with explanations given in the Glossary and, where appropriate, in the text, to enable you to understand different manufacturers' patterns.

☐ All instructions are for use on single bed machines from the simplest hand tensioned machine (eg. Bond) to electronic machines. Where differences occur they are stated.

☐ Refer to the two lists of common problems, one for stocking stitch, the other for patterned knitting, for help when difficulties arise.

☐ Tips in the text offer suggestions and explanations, so that some common misunderstandings can be avoided.

☐ Like most craft skills, machine knitting improves with practice, so keep trying. When things just don't seem to be going right, take a break. Ask someone else to read the instructions to you if you do get stuck. Even if they know nothing of machine knitting, it will help you if they read through to the end of the section!

Just enjoy knitting. Don't worry about taking time to learn or about making mistakes; everybody has been there before – and some mistakes have become very attractive garments! When family and friends have had their share of your new all-absorbing interest, please knit something for yourself.

THE KNITTING MACHINE

INTRODUCING KNITTING MACHINES

The knitting machine is a collection of latched needles which are held an equal distance apart in a frame or 'bed'. Knitting is produced when the needles are moved through the stitches by the 'carriage', a kind of channelled platform carrying yarn, which is passed backwards and forwards across the bed, making each stitch of equal size.

SINGLE BED MACHINES

As the name implies these machines have a single bed of needles. The basic stitch they knit is stocking stitch. The fabric produced has one side 'knit' and the other side 'purl'. The knit, or plain side is smooth. The purl, or ridged side is sometimes known as the 'wrong' side, but attractive stitch patterns are made on both this and the knit side of the fabric. On a single bed machine the fabric is formed with the purl side facing the operator.

DOUBLE BED MACHINES

These machines have two beds of needles joined so that the hooks of the needles are opposite each other. True ribs are knitted when needles from both beds carry stitches, for example, in a knit one stitch, purl one stitch simple rib, alternate needles from each bed hold the stitches across a row. Stocking stitch can still be knitted but by using one bed only.

RIBBER

This is a bed of needles which can be attached to a single bed machine to form a double bed machine. These are available for most single bed machines, therefore for beginners it is usually easier to learn machine knitting on a single bed machine and add a ribber later.

MACHINE TYPES

Single and double bed knitting machines are classified into three main types according to the distance between the individual needles. The closer the needles are positioned together, the thinner the yarn that can be used.

FINE GAUGE

These are used to knit very thin yarns and produce a fabric which is similar to commercial knitware.

STANDARD GAUGE

These are used to knit yarns of thicknesses equivalent to a hand knit 2, 3 or 4 ply. (Thinner yarn can be used but usually 2 or 3 strands together. Thicker yarns may be knitted on alternate needles.)

CHUNKY

On these machines the needles are spaced apart up to twice the distance of those on the standard gauge machines and so will knit 'Double Knit' (DK), Aran and Chunky yarns.

STITCH PATTERNING

There are several ways of working decorative stitch patterns when knitting by machine, depending on what type of machine is being used.

MANUAL SELECTION

Stitch patterns are made by moving needles individually and transferring stitches using hand held tools. These are usually the less expensive machines.

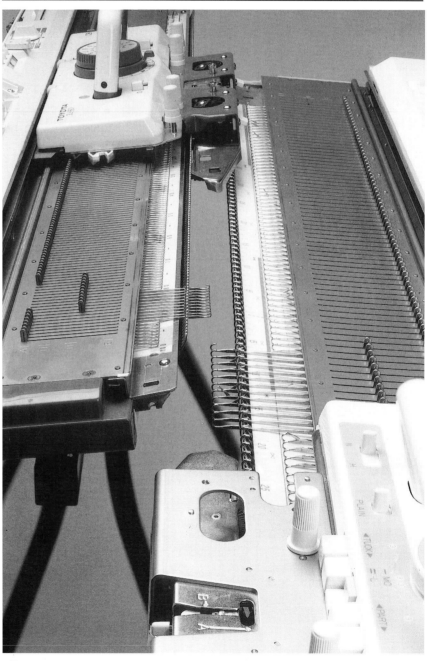

Close up showing the difference in needle spacing between (left) a Toyota 901 standard gauge knitting machine and (right) a Brother 260 Chunky.

PUSH BUTTON SELECTION

Buttons are pressed to set up the pattern sequence. At the start of each row the needles are then selected along the needle bed by operating a lever. The pattern is usually repeated over 8 to 12 stitches.

PUNCHCARD

A card carrying the stitch pattern, which is represented by holes and blanks, is fed into the machine. This card moves row by row as the knitting progresses, automatically selecting the needles. Most modern machines use a rotating card. Pattern repeats of 2, 3, 4, 6, 8, 12 and 24 stitches can be selected.

ELECTRONIC PATTERNING

Machines with this type of patterning scan a plastic sheet on which a stitch pattern of from 2 to 60 stitches wide and from 1 to 150 rows long is drawn. A built-in microchip enables this pattern to be expanded up to a maximum size of from 2 to 120 stitches wide and from 2 to 300 rows long. (The Brother 950 also has a built-in memory of over 500 stitch patterns.)

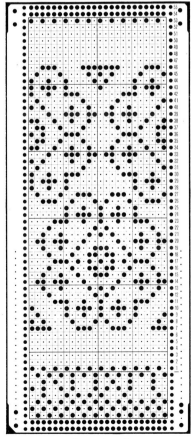

A punchcard

One of the standard pattern sheets from a Brother 910 Electronic.

CHOOSING A MACHINE

Before buying a machine, try to see and hear one being operated. Machines are noisy, and need space to be operated efficiently. Decide on the type of knitting you want to do, for example, with thick or thin yarn. Many hand knitters choose the fine and standard gauge machines and continue to hand knit the thicker yarns, although to be able to knit a thick sweater in an evening using the 'chunky' machine appeals to others.

Price will also influence your choice. Cheaper machines have less mechanical aids to knitting stitch patterns, so it takes longer to knit patterned garments. However, such machines can be used very effectively to make stunningly original garments. More expensive machines with mechanical and electronic pattern selection take longer to learn to use, but, after practice, it is possible to knit a patterned garment much more rapidly than with one of the simpler machines.

To help you make your choice try to see as many machines working as possible. Ask your local knitting club or Adult Education class; most knitters are happy to talk about machine knitting.

POINTS TO REMEMBER

Whichever machine you decide to buy, do ask about spares, after-sales service and whether the model is due to be updated. Many manufacturers make additional attachments and it is often worth asking if these can be included in a total package as very often a worthwhile saving can be made over buying the attachments separately afterwards.

Second-hand machines are advertised in national machine knitting magazines. They are worth considering as they can be bargains; some are often little used, while others are sold by experienced knitters who are buying more advanced machines. Before buying check that spares are still obtainable for the machine and an instruction book is included. Examine the machine and check that the needles are straight (one or two bent needles are easily replaced), and that the carriage moves freely. Ask for a demonstration and then try it yourself. Check that all the tools are included – look in the instruction book.

But remember, whether you buy a new or a second-hand machine, be prepared to look at several machines before you find the right one.

YARNS

There is a wide choice of yarn, both in fibre content and construction, available to the machine knitter.

FIBRES

Man Made: Acrylic (Courtelle), Viscose, Nylon.
Natural: Wool, Cotton, Silk, Linen, Animal hairs.
The most popular yarn for the beginner to use when machine knitting is made from acrylic fibre. The yarn runs smoothly through the machine and forms an attractive 'woolly' fabric, which does not change shape when washed and requires no pressing. It is also inexpensive to buy. Nylon on its own can be too springy to knit with but if mixed with acrylic fibres it gives a strong yarn which knits easily. Natural fibres, when spun for the machine knitter, are usually easy to knit with but require careful laundering and are generally more expensive than acrylic yarn. Many combinations of natural and man made fibres are spun into yarn and sold for the domestic machine knitter. Yarn labelled as being suitable for machine knitting is a safe buy.

'PLY'

The term 'ply' refers to the number of strands or 'plies' twisted together to make the thickness of yarn. Almost all yarns used for machine knitting are made up of at least 2 strands. The thickness of the individual strands governs the thickness of the yarn; however the common name used to describe yarn type, i.e. 3 ply, 4 ply, indicates thickness rather than the number of stands and is taken from hand knitting usage.

FANCY YARNS

These come in several forms such as 'boucle', slub, chenille, hairy (mohair) and crimp, and where sold for the domestic machines will knit well and often surprisingly easily despite their appearance. They consist either of a single type of fibre or a mixture of different types.

INDUSTRIAL YARNS

These can be natural or man made fibres which are available as 'end of line'

Opposite: *An indication of the immense variety of yarns available.*

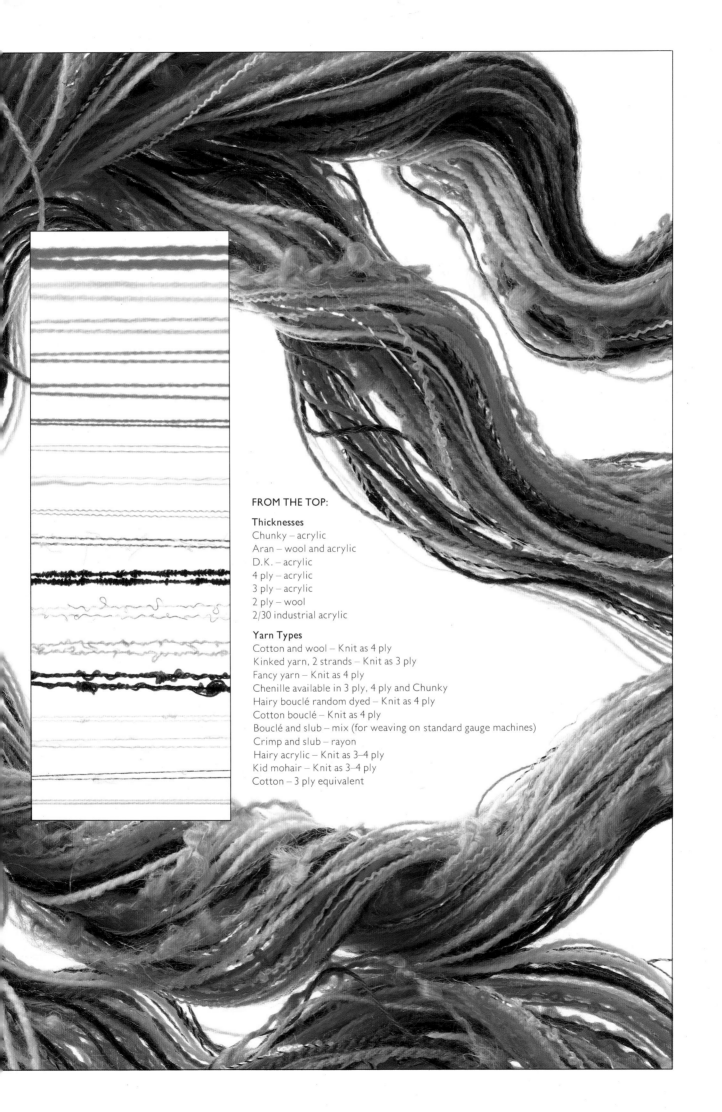

FROM THE TOP:

Thicknesses
Chunky – acrylic
Aran – wool and acrylic
D.K. – acrylic
4 ply – acrylic
3 ply – acrylic
2 ply – wool
2/30 industrial acrylic

Yarn Types
Cotton and wool – Knit as 4 ply
Kinked yarn, 2 strands – Knit as 3 ply
Fancy yarn – Knit as 4 ply
Chenille available in 3 ply, 4 ply and Chunky
Hairy bouclé random dyed – Knit as 4 ply
Cotton bouclé – Knit as 4 ply
Bouclé and slub – mix (for weaving on standard gauge machines)
Crimp and slub – rayon
Hairy acrylic – Knit as 3–4 ply
Kid mohair – Knit as 3–4 ply
Cotton – 3 ply equivalent

bargains for the domestic machine knitter. Some fine 'industrial' acrylic yarn is obtainable in repeatable colours and is known as '2/30's', a commercial term which is the equivalent of 'ply' in hand knitting. When knitted on a standard gauge machine 3 thicknesses used together will give a thickness amost equivalent to '4 ply'. These yarns are inexpensive and a little goes a long way, however as they are not as easy to use as a single thickness yarn, extra care is needed when using them, but they are certainly worth considering for a knitter with some experience. The exact fibre content is often difficult to ascertain so it is always necessary to knit samples and experiment before committing yourself to knitting a whole garment.

TIP
□ When using 3 thicknesses of fine yarn use 3 separate balls of yarn and thread them individually through the tension mast.

CONED YARNS
The banded brand-named cones prepared for the domestic machine knitter provide a reliable yarn for the beginner. Coned yarn has the advantage of being in a continuous length with the central cardboard cone supporting the yarn so allowing it to run evenly and smoothly as you knit. This is a very important consideration when knitting at speed. A cone of yarn is also cheaper than buying the equivalent weight in balled yarn.

HAND KNITTING YARN
This can be used on a knitting machine but you should work from the centre of the ball; otherwise the ball is jerked as the yarn is used, causing uneven knitting.

TIP
□ When knitting from a ball of yarn, join the end of the ball you are knitting to the beginning of the next ball with a knot, then, at the start of a row, pull the yarn and knot through the tension arm and carriage and hold down below the needle bed. Continue to knit, leaving the ends to be neatened off later. This is quicker than re-threading every time a new ball is started.

WASTE YARN
'Waste yarn' is the term used to describe yarn used to hold stitches at the start of hems, or where a closed edge is not required because it is to be finished by an alternative method. The waste yarn holds the stitches and is later removed and thrown away. Remember

that any oddments of yarn may be used, for example re-wound test pieces of knitting.

RE-USING YARN
When re-knitting previously used yarn it is important to remove the kinks, otherwise uneven stitches result. The yarn should be unravelled and made into skeins or hanks. These should then be washed or steamed, dried and then re-wound into balls – ready to be used again.

TIP
□ When re-using yarn consisting of several lengths wound into one ball, join the lengths with a section of contrast coloured yarn. The join can then be spotted before it is knitted, and even if it is not it will still be easier to unpick the stitches knitted in the contrast yarn than it would be to pick up the dropped stitches which would result from the yarn running out before the end of the row.

GETTING READY TO KNIT

Collect together a pencil, note pad, tape measure, ruler and pocket calculator. Most patterns for garments use centimetres for giving measurements within the patterns, as do the charting devices which are built in to some machines.

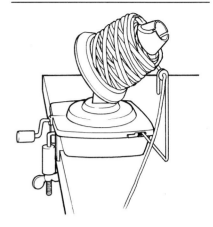

A woolwinder winds the yarn into balls.

TIP
□ If you find centimetres confusing, and still think in inches, then find a tape measure with inches and centimetres on the same side of the tape. This will help you to become accustomed to centimetres (cm).

A woolwinder is also an essential extra. It is inexpensive to buy and is used to re-wind yarn quickly and easily. It is quicker than winding by hand and produces an evenly wound ball that runs freely when knitting.

For practice choose two yarns of contrasting colours in 4 ply acrylic for standard gauge machines or DK acrylic for chunky machines.

TIP
□ It is often quicker to unravel, rewind and re-knit a piece of knitting than to try to correct a mistake.

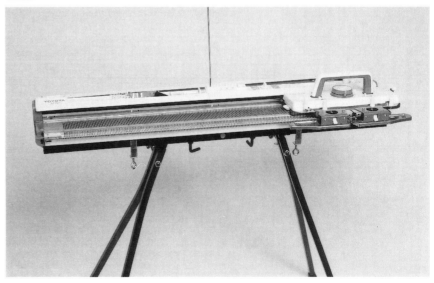

Toyota tilt table with a machine.

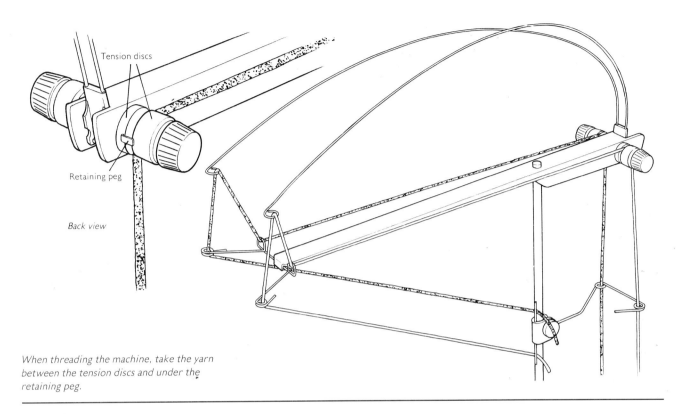

Tension discs

Retaining peg

Back view

When threading the machine, take the yarn between the tension discs and under the retaining peg.

Before starting to knit, the machine must be clamped to a table, to hold it securely whilst knitting. Special machine tables can be purchased which are the length of and a little wider than the machine. This has the advantage that a cone of yarn, placed on the floor behind the machine, when threaded into the machine can run freely and so produce even knitting. Toyota make a special 'tilt' table for their range of machines. This is invaluable when the ribber is attached, but can also be used if starting with a single bed alone. If possible keep the machine set up – you are more likely to practice if the machine is ready for use. Cover the needle bed to keep the machine dust-free and to protect the needles, especially if small children are about, as the hooks are very sharp. Check the clamps from time to time, as they can work loose and a damaged machine can be expensive to repair, and it is also painful if it damages you.

Assemble the machine following your instruction manual. Do not be alarmed by the number of pages; the instructions are usually very clear. Just take it step by step.

When threading the machine it is important that the yarn is taken between the tension discs and under the retaining peg in the yarn tension arm assembly. This peg prevents the yarn from jumping out from the discs when knitting. The discs control the tension on

the yarn and the antenna-like wires maintain the tension as the carriage moves to and fro when knitting. When the yarn is threaded at the correct tension the wires are pulled into a D-shaped curve. This shape is altered by tightening or loosening the yarn tension disc screws.

TIP
☐ *Clip the end of the yarn into the holder on the yarn tension arm rod, then check the yarn tension by pulling the yarn back down behind the machine so that the wires are curved down towards the end of the yarn guide. When released the yarn should be drawn up through the tension discs to form a D-shape. Adjust if necessary. If your machine does not have any form of yarn tension assembly it will be necessary to pull back the yarn just before the carriage starts to move across the working needles. This will have to be done on every row, when using the Bond machine for example.*

READY TO KNIT
There are several methods of casting on. One will be given in your instruction book as a preferred method for your particular model. When you have mastered this, look at the alternative techniques offered on the following pages.

ABBREVIATIONS

RHS	Right-hand side
LHS	Left-hand side
Dec	Decrease
Inc	Increase
× 10	Inc/Dec 10 times in all
× 8	Inc/Dec 8 times in all
× 7	Inc/Dec 7 times in all, and so on.
HP	Holding position
WP	Work position
UWP	Upper work position
NWP	Non work position (See also Needle positions', p. 24.)
MT	(Main tension) stitch size
MY	Main yarn
RC	Row counter
DK	Double knit
st	stitch or stitches
cm	centimetre or centimetres
in	inch or inches

(See also pp. 28, 45.)

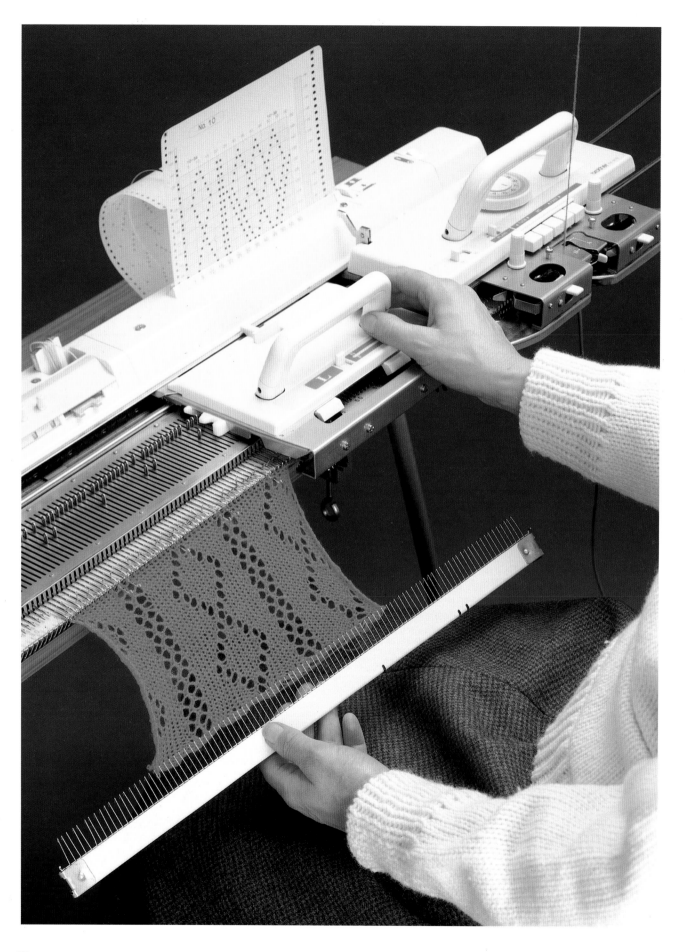

GLOSSARY

THE CARRIAGE

This consists of two parts: the main section and the sinker plate assembly.

The main section: This is moved over the needle bed by its handle. On the under side of the main section is a series of cams and plates. These are operated by levers and dials located on the upper side, which form channels through which the needle butts pass to make different patterns and sizes of stitch. On some machines the main section of the carriage also carries the needle selection mechanism.

The sinker plate assembly, or arm: This is the front section of the carriage which sticks out in front of the sinker posts. It carries the yarn threading guides as well as the brushes and wheels which push the yarn when knitting. It is held in position on the main section by two thumb screws.

TIP

□ *The brushes located underneath the sinker plate assembly should spin round freely. If they do not then unscrew the centre brush screw and remove the brushes. Yarn strands collect round the brush spindles resulting in the brushes not moving properly so that the yarn is not fed into the hooks. Clean the brushes and the spindles and replace the brushes.*

Lace carriage

This is an additional carriage used only for lace knitting. It lifts and pushes the needles in such a way as to transfer the stitch on to the adjacent needle – often quite alarming the first time lace knitting is tried. There are two types of lace carriage, the first only selects and transfers the stitches, while the second selects, transfers and knits all in one row. (Some of the more recent models of machine are able to knit lace without a second carriage.)

Tension dial on carriage

This dial should more accurately be called the 'stitch size selection' dial as it sets the distance over which the needles are moved back as they pull the

Opposite: Lace knitting on a Brother Electronic 910 machine. Both carriages are used.

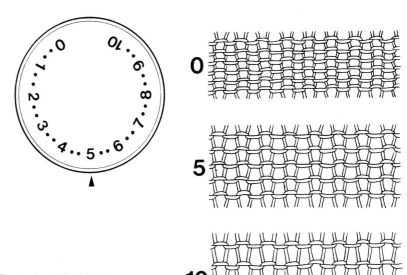

The tension dial selects the stitch size. The dots represent intermediate stitch sizes; 31 stitch sizes are available for use here.

loop of yarn caught in the hook. The further they are moved back the bigger the loop of the stitch. Settings are given in whole numbers with two intermediate stitch sizes marked by dots. The stitch size setting is often written as a whole number followed by point one or two, for example, 6.2 or 6 followed by two dots. This indicates a setting position of 6 and then 2 places or 'clicks' more on the dial.

All manufacturers use similar methods of numbering tension dials but the numbers can represent different stitch sizes. This means that a Knitmaster owner using the same yarn as a Brother machine owner may have to select a different number on the tension dial in order to achieve the same sized stitch.

CAST ON COMBS

Combs are supplied by two manufacturers – Brother and Toyota. They consist of a metal and plastic bar with metal hooks along one side. The hooks hold the yarn to assist in making the first row of stitches when starting to knit. The Brother comb hooks on to the yarn between every needle whereas the Toyota comb hooks the yarn only between every other needle. The combs can also be used as extra weights.

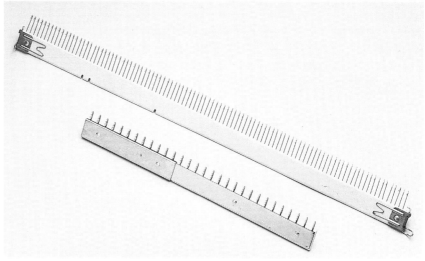

Cast on combs: *(top) Brother, (bottom) Toyota.*

CROCHET HOOK

The crochet hook end of this tool can be used in the conventional manner, and the point at the opposite end is used to catch a dropped stitch, and to hold it before picking up with a transfer or latch tool and replacing on the needle.

EXTENSION RAILS

Where machines use both a lace carriage and main carriage together when knitting lace, for example, most Brother and Toyota machines, one carriage will rest on the extension rail while the other carriage is working. The main carriage knits the stitches that have been transferred by the lace carriage. These rails require extra space when used but it is not necessary to have them in place permanently.

LATCH TOOL OR TAPPIT TOOL

This tool looks like the hook section of a needle mounted in a handle. It is used to knit up dropped stitches or to pull one stitch through another when casting off.

NEEDLES

All modern machines have latched needles which have a butt, shank and hook.

The shank: This should be straight.

The butt: This protrudes between slots in the needle bed. This is the part of the needle which is moved by the carriage when knitting a stitch.

The hook: This carries the stitch and catches the yarn when the next stitch is knitted. If the hook becomes twisted the stitch will not knit properly.

The latch: This moves backwards and forwards as the yarn is caught then pulled through the stitch. It must move freely and close over the tip of the hook.

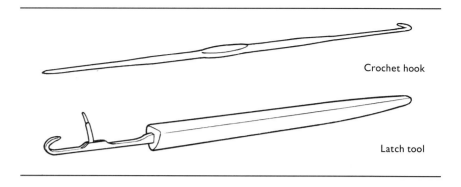

Crochet hook

Latch tool

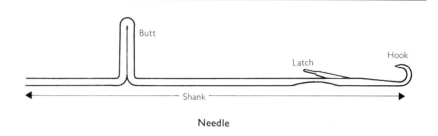

Needle

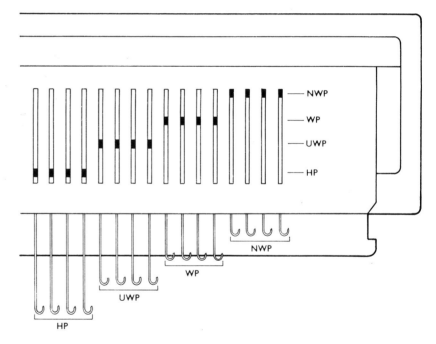

The four main needle positions as referred to in this book.

		BROTHER	KNITMASTER	TOYOTA	SINGER
Needle position	Abbreviation				
Non-working position	NWP	A	A	A	A
Working position	WP	B	B	B	B
Upper working position	UWP	D	C	D	D
Holding position	HP	E	D	E	F

□ *To check if the needles are straight pull all the needles forwards to their furthest extent. Bent shanks show easily. Brush the latches open so that they lie back evenly along the shanks. Close the latches and check that the spoonlike tip of the latch lies over the tip of the hook. Refer to your instruction book and change any bent or damaged needles.*

Needle positions

Manufacturers differ in their use of lettering to indicate needle positions on the needle bed. Four main positions are referred to in this book: NWP, WP, UWP and HP. (See table p. 24.)

NWP needles do not knit.

WP needles knit stocking stitch. Some machines knit stitch patterns in this position, for example, 'tuck' stitches on Brother machines.

UWP needles are the patterning needles on some machines. Needles will also knit back to WP when pushed to this position from HP. (If the needles were moved directly back to WP the stitches would fall off the needles.)

HP needles do not knit when the 'Hold' lever is set. (Some manual pattern selection machines do not have a 'Hold' setting lever and so the needles will remain in this position without knitting until they are pushed back to the UWP – as in the Bond machines.)
   HP can be used when knitting patterned stitches or shaping garments.

NEEDLE PROTECTION STRIP

A numbered strip which lies behind the sinker posts and under the needle hooks. It marks the number of the needles either side of the central 'O', and is used to help count the needles or stitches in use.

NEEDLE PUSHERS

Most single bed machines are supplied with a I × I needle pusher. This has a long, straight edge which is used to move the needles to working position on the bed. The I × I tooth-like edge enables alternate needles to be moved. The needles are moved or 'pushed' by placing the pusher behind or in front of the needle butts. Extra needle pushers can be purchased if required for different needle arrangements, for example, 2 × I, 2 × 2, 3 × I, etc.

TIP
□ *Try putting the needles in the various working positions, move the carriage*

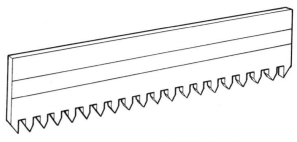

I × I Needle pusher

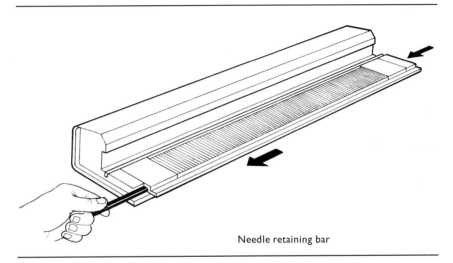

Needle retaining bar

across without yarn and see what happens to the needles. (See 'Holding', p. 66.)

NEEDLE RETAINING BAR

A strip of metal and foam used to hold the needles in place, located under the front edge of the needle bed. When pushed out from either end of the machine the needles are released and can then be removed. New needles are inserted and the bar pushed back into position.

NYLON CORD, RAVEL CORD OR CAST-ON CORD

This is a length of nylon cord, usually white, which is used to start knitting, hold stitches or separate waste yarn from the main yarn when knitting. It is very strong and needs to be kept free of knots. This book uses the term 'nylon cord' throughout the instructions.

TIP
□ *To keep the cord knot-free it can be kept wound round the indented handle of your cleaning brush. If you do not have this type of brush use a small oblong shaped piece of wood or cardboard with sections cut out on the short sides. This will hold the cord and can be kept with the other machine tools.*

RIGHT HAND SIDE (RHS) OR LEFT HAND SIDE (LHS)

Knitting machines can be operated by right- and left-handed users equally well because both hands need to be used when machine knitting. Most machines will start to knit with the carriage at either side of the needle bed

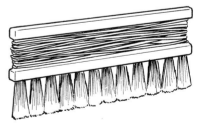

Brush with holder

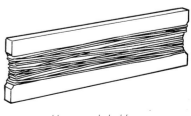

Home-made holder

This Fair Isle slipover (pp. 92–3) has been knitted using random-dyed wool for an attractive and easy-to-achieve result. The school jumper is an ever popular knitting project, made by adapting the round neck jumper with set-in sleeves (pp. 84–5) to a V neck jumper (p. 88).

although some instruction books give the impression that all settings have to be carried out at a specific side.

However it is necessary to start knitting with the carriage at a particular side in some instances, for example, when knitting lace. Carriage position instructions are given in this book, but the settings may be reversed and the opposite end of the machine used provided that all instructions are reversed.

For example, where instructions for the 'e-wrap' cast-on are given (see p. 33) with the carriage at RHS and wrapping direction from left to right you can reverse the instruction so that when the carriage is at LHS the wrapping direction will be from right to left.

ROW COUNTER (RC)

A counting device which is operated as the carriage moves backwards and forwards across the needle bed.

SINKER POST, SINKER PEGS OR SINKER GATE

These are a row of metal pegs along the front edge of the machine, which push the yarn down between the stitches when knitting. Some machines have closed sinker posts or a sinker gate. In this case a continuous metal strip closes the top of the sinker posts. Chunky machines often use this system.

SPRAY WAX

A silicone spray which can be used when the solid disc of wax is insufficient.

TIP
□ *Spray wax can be sprayed on to the cone as you knit. Further applications are made when the carriage becomes heavy and stiff, dragging across the bed. However if the cone is generously sprayed with the wax in a plastic bag, and the bag is sealed and left overnight, then the yarn will be more evenly and efficiently waxed.*

STITCH SIZE

Choice of stitch size

When using a new yarn or machine you will need to try out several stitch size settings on the tension dial before you select the one which is right for your proposed garment. A thin yarn knitted on a large stitch size produces a soft fabric, whereas a smaller stitch with the same yarn will produce a firmer fabric. There is no 'correct' stitch size for a particular yarn. The choice is yours and depends on the final effect you wish to achieve.

Large stitch size 7

Medium stitch size 6

2 rows biggest stitch size – marker row

Small stitch size 5

Choice of stitch size

STITCH SIZE ABBREVIATIONS

By convention machine knitting pattern writers indicate the stitch sizes used by reference to the 'MT' (Main Tension)

MT — This is the *main stitch size* used when knitting a garment.

MT − (minus) a number indicates the amount by which the MT number should be reduced when a smaller stitch size is required. *For example*, if MT is set at 8 then MT − 3 would indicate a setting on the tension dial of 5.

MT + (plus) a number requires a larger stitch size to be used. *For example*, MT + 2 where the MT is set at 8 would indicate a setting of 10 on the tension dial.

TIP
□ *To test for stitch size, cast on over 10 to 20 needles. Start by using the smallest stitch size you think practical (a low number on the tension dial). Knit 20 rows, then knit 2 rows in the largest stitch size. Return to your starting stitch size and increase it by one whole number. Knit 20 rows and again the 2 rows on the largest stitch size. Continue repeating this process until you have tried all the stitch sizes that you may wish to use.*

Remove the knitting from the machine. Wash or press the sample and then decide which stitch size produces the results that you require. Remember to make a note of the stitch size you have tried.

TENSION

This is the number of rows and stitches worked over a measured area of knitting. It is the information needed to knit a correctly sized garment. (See 'Tension', pp. 47–49.)

TENSION MAST AND TENSION ARM

This is the mechanism used to control the tension of the yarn being fed to the machine when knitting. It is found on most machines at the top of the yarn tension unit rod. It consists of two discs held together by a spring, the pressure of which is adjusted by the tension arm dial screw. The tightness of the screw controls the rate at which the yarn runs throughout the discs and so directly affects the size of the stitch formed.

TRANSFER TOOLS

Most machines are provided with three transfer tools, and these are used to move stitches on the machine.

The easiest way to use a transfer tool is to hold it with the palm of your hand facing upwards and the tool lying across the palm and index finger. Place the thumb on the flat part of the central handle. When transferring stitches try to keep the hand tool in the same plane as the needles to reduce the chance of stitches sliding off the tool. It is also helpful when transferring stitches to hold the knitted fabric back against the sinker posts with the other hand.

WAX

This is used to smooth down hairs on the yarn, making it easier to knit. Some machines have a peg on the tension arm assembly on which a wax disc can be placed. The yarn is then drawn over the wax as it is knitted.

WEIGHTS

Single bed machines use hinged claw weights to hold the knitted fabric down whilst knitting. This is particularly helpful when:
1. Patterning, where the edge stitches tend to move forward along the needle.
2. Shaping, for example, to prevent the decreasing on a raglan sleeve from pulling tight.
3. Making a multiple increase, to hold the new stitches knitted down.
4. Knitting the first side of the neck edge of a jumper.
5. Hung on to a cast-on comb to give extra weight.

For addition terms see 'Optional Extras' on p. 120.

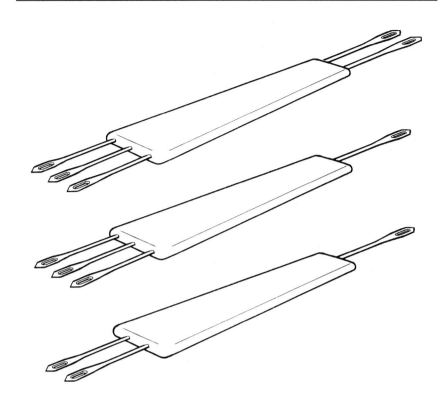

Three transfer tools, which usually come with the machine.

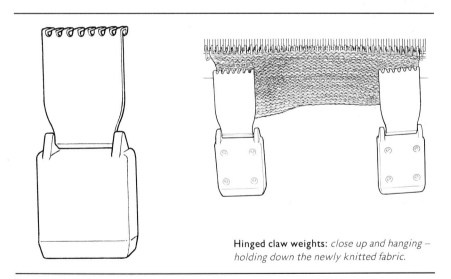

Hinged claw weights: *close up and hanging – holding down the newly knitted fabric.*

TECHNIQUES

METHODS OF CASTING ON

OPEN-EDGE CAST-ON
Using nylon cord

Machine note
The machine must have open sinker posts.

This edge is not closed and will unravel.

Uses
For knitting trial pieces, tension swatches and knitting with waste yarn for welts. This edge is knitted very quickly but is not suitable for finished garments.

Method
Thread tension mast and carriage and secure free end under machine. (*Hint:* the clamp is often a convenient anchor point.)
Bring forward required number of needles to working position (WP). Knit across 1 row. The yarn forms a zig-zag between the needle hooks and the sinker posts.
Take the nylon cord and lay it over the zig-zag yarn, placing it in front of the needle hooks and behind the sinker posts. Hold both ends of the nylon cord together very firmly down below the machine.
Move the carriage across, slowly, for 1 row. The nylon cord forms the base of the stitch, so that a loop of yarn can be drawn through to make a stitch. Continue holding the nylon cord for a further 6 to 8 rows.
Pull out the cord and continue knitting normally.

TIP
☐ *If the first row knitted over the nylon cord does not knit properly, it could be because the nylon cord was not held tightly enough or that there are too many stitches to be held. Start again, and this time pull about every 10th needle to HP, making sure that the needle passes over the cord, then, holding the cord ends very firmly, knit 1 row. The stitches now have a base and will knit normally.*

With most modern-day machines the needles return to the working position after the carriage is moved across. If the needles do not return to working position after knitting the row, remember to check that the machine is set for normal knitting.

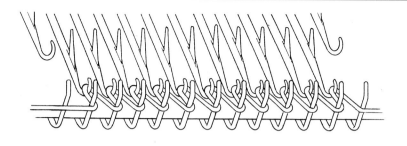

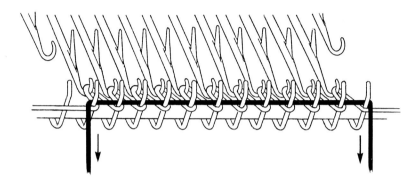

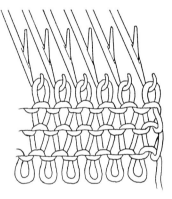

Open-edge cast-on (from top): **1**. *Zigzag made by* MY. **2**. *Nylon cord forms the base of the stitch; hold down firmly.* **3**. *Finished edge.*

WOVEN-EDGE CAST-ON

Machine note
The machine must have a facility for weaving.

This edge has a single length of yarn running through the bottom row of stitches so will not unravel. However, as the stitches are only held by a single length of yarn, it is not strong enough for a permanent finish.

Uses
For edges of garments where the stitches, held by the thread, are to be picked up after the main knitting is completed in order to knit a hem. When stitch samples are kept for reference, or for an edge that is to be gathered.

Method
Push the number of needles required to WP, then push every alternate needle to HP. Set the machine to weave.
Thread the yarn through the carriage, but – instead of securing the free end – take it under the carriage and up over the needles. Lie the yarn against the sinker posts over the needle shanks. Holding the free end lightly, move the carriage across the needles allowing the free end to be drawn into the knitting as the needles start to knit. Stitches with a proper base are formed on alternate needles and the needles which carry only a loop of yarn at this stage will form stitches on the following row.

After 8 to 10 rows, cancel the weave settings. Set machine for normal knitting.

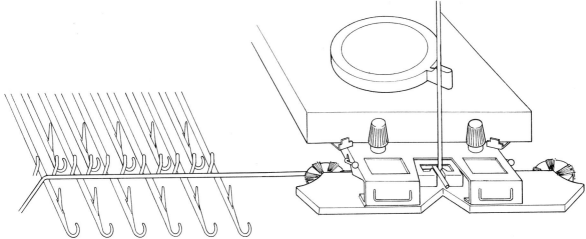

Woven edge cast-on: *Needles and yarn position.*

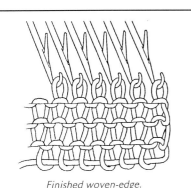

Finished woven-edge.

TIP
□ *If a loop forms at the start of the row this could be because the yarn has caught under the carriage. This can be avoided if the yarn is pulled back just before the carriage starts to knit.*

'e-WRAP' CAST-ON

This method forms a closed edge.

Uses
As a finished edge when hems are not required, when a sewn border or a crocheted edge is added after the knitting is completed, when several stitches need to be added at the beginning of a row to shape the knitting.

Method
Push all the required needles to HP. Place the carriage at the RHS. Take the yarn leading from the tension mast in your right hand, hold the free end with your left hand, and then, with your right hand and starting at the LHS, take the yarn under the first needle then over the top of the needle and back down the left side of the needle, then back under the needle. This process forms a letter 'e'. Take the yarn to the right and bring it up between the second and third needles, over the top of the second needle and down between the first and second needles to make the next stitch. Repeat the process. Once 2 or 3 stitches have been formed hold the stitches back against the sinker posts with the left index finger. Keep repeating the process to the last needle. Thread the yarn into the carriage.

Pull the yarn back through the tension mast to adjust the yarn tension, knit one row then check that all the stitches have knitted.

TIPS
□ *If the stitches have not knitted correctly, the 'e-wrap' casting-on may have been too tight, so try again, working it more loosely.*
□ *If the second (the next) row does not knit correctly, start again, but before knitting the second row, push all the needles to HP, making sure that the cast-on row is pushed evenly back against the sinker posts. Repeat this for 2 to 3 rows, then continue knitting normally.*

LATCH TOOL CAST-ON

Tool
Latch tool.

Uses
This provides a firm, neat chain edge suitable for a permanent finished edge.

When the main knitting is in stocking stitch, the edge tends to curl. This effect can be reduced by working a

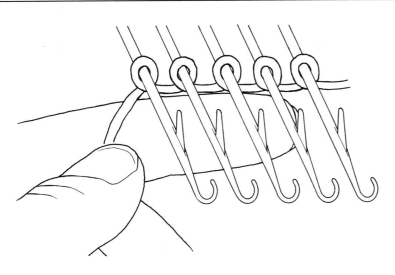

'e-wrap' cast-on with finger holding wrapped stitches in position.

crocheted edge when the garment is finished, which adds extra weight.

Method

Put the required number of needles into HP. Make a slip knot and place on to the shank of the latch tool, behind the latch. At the opposite end to the carriage, hold the latch tool under the needles, with the yarn coming down from the tension mast outside the needles.

Move the latch tool under the first needle, then push it up between the first and second needles. Hold the latch open. Catch the yarn in the hook and pull a loop through the slip knot making a stitch in the latch tool hook. This will form a loop over the first needle for the first stitch.

Move the tool and stitch down and under the second needle. Now holding the stitch on the shank behind the latch, bring the latch tool back up between the second and third needles. Catch the yarn and pull the loop through the stitch.

Repeat this procedure until the last needle, then slip the last loop formed on to the hook of the last needle. Thread the yarn into the carriage and knit across.

TIP

□ *Hold the yarn from the tension wire above the needles as there is less chance of the stitches becoming unravelled if a loop is dropped. Try not to make the stitch loops too tight.*

A slash neck jumper in plain stocking stitch is the first jumper to knit (pp. 52–6), but one to knit again and again.

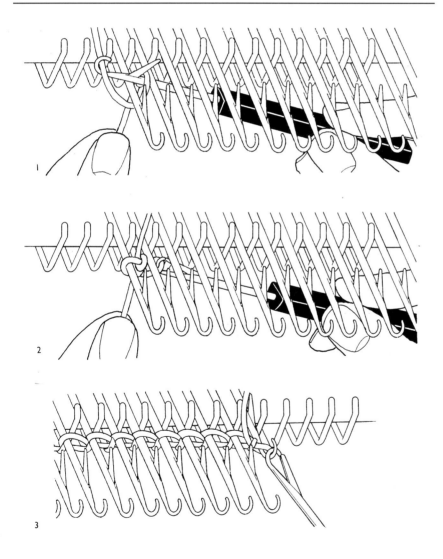

Latch tool cast-on: *Method* **1.** *Making 1st stitch.* **2.** *Loop pulled under needle.* **3.** *Loop put onto end.*

PRACTICE

Machine note
With a chunky machine use a double-knit yarn over 20 needles and stitch tension setting of 4 to 5. With a standard-gauge machine use a 4 ply yarn and a stitch tension setting of 6 or 7.

Cast on using one of the methods given and knit 10 to 15 rows. Break the yarn, unthread yarn from the carriage, then take the carriage across the needles so that the knitting falls off. This is the easiest way to 'cast off'.

TIP
□ *If the knitting falls off unintentionally when you are knitting, check that the yarn has been correctly threaded into the carriage and that it is running freely.*

METHODS OF CASTING OFF

Casting off is not always necessary at the end of each piece of knitting. Waste yarn can be used to hold the stitches until required, for example, when shoulder stitches are to be knitted together to form the seam, or neckbands added. Casting off gives a firm edge.

SIMPLE CASTING OFF

Tool
Single-pronged transfer tool

Method
Casting off is worked from the end of the knitting nearest the carriage.

Take the first stitch nearest to the carriage from the needle on to the transfer tool, slip this stitch on to the next needle.
Pull the needle towards you, making both stitches move back behind the latch. Take the yarn under, then over, the needle into the hook.
With your thumb on the needle-butt, push the needle back knitting the two stitches together.
The new stitch is then transferred in the same way to the adjacent needle and knitted off as before.

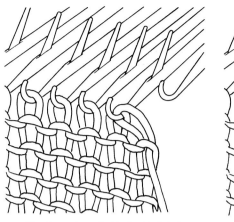

Simple casting off: *Method 1. Stitch transferred to adjacent needle.*

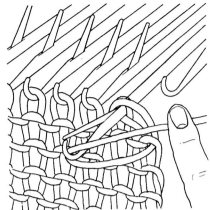

2. Yarn placed in needle hook.

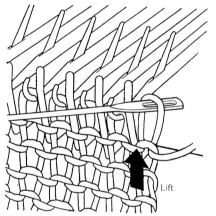

3. Use the transfer tool to move the stitch behind the sinker post.

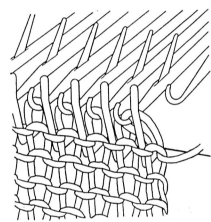

4. Place the stitch onto the next needle. Cast off as before.

Repeat this process until one stitch remains. Break off the yarn, secure the end of the yarn still threaded through tension mast under the clip on the tension mast; then pull the other end through the last stitch. Fasten off by making a knot.

CASTING OFF BEHIND SINKER POSTS

Machine note
The machine must have open sinker posts.

Tool
Single-pronged transfer tool.

This is a similar technique to the first method but produces an evenly spaced, looser cast-off edge which is easier to sew up when finishing the garment.

Method
Take the first stitch off on to the single-pronged transfer tool as before, but – instead of bringing the stitch out towards you in front of the sinker post – lay the stitch behind the sinker post before transferring it to the next needle.

TIP
□ *The easiest way to transfer this stitch is to place the tip of the transfer tool on the needle bed, allowing the stitch to slip towards the eye of the tool. Hold the tip down firmly, lift the shank of the tool over the adjacent sinker post; the stitch is now lying behind the sinker post. Lift the tool and place the stitch on to the hook of the next needle.*

Continue to cast off as for the simple cast-off method, but place each stitch behind the sinker posts. When the casting off is complete the knitting will still be attached to the machine but can easily be lifted off.

LATCH TOOL CAST-OFF

Tool

Latch tool.

The latch tool is used to make a chain edge which, with practice, is quickly done and forms a very neat finished edge. The last row of knitting must be worked in a larger stitch size than the main knitting, usually 2 to 3 whole numbers greater on the 'tension dial'. This consideration limits the occasions on which this method can be used.

Method

Start at the opposite end to the carriage. Knit the last row before casting off using a larger stitch size. Hook the first stitch from the first needle on to the latch tool. Slide the stitch down the shank of the tool behind the latch. Hold the latch open with the index finger. Take the 2nd stitch into the hook of the latch tool and lift it off the needle, at the same time, with the other hand gently pull downwards on the knitted fabric, keeping the stitches on the needles.

When the second stitch is in the hook lift the index finger, pull the latch tool back, allowing the stitch behind the latch to slip forward, closing the latch and so passing over the second stitch and off the tool. Slip the remaining stitch in the hook behind the latch and repeat the process until all the stitches are cast off.

The last stitch is finished by breaking the yarn and pulling the free end through the last stitch, making a knot.

Tip

□ *When casting off a lot of stitches it helps to have the hand holding the latch tool held at an angle of 45 degrees to the needles, and to move your chair along as you work down the needle bed.*

LOOSER LATCH TOOL CAST-OFF

This is used when knitting with a large stitch size to avoid too tight a cast-off edge. It is done by working an extra chain stitch between the existing stitches. This method of casting off must start at the same side of the work as the carriage. The yarn is knitted in as the cast-off is worked.

Method

At the same end as the carriage take the first stitch on to the shank of the latch tool. Holding the latch open, catch the main yarn into the hook. Close the latch and pull a loop of yarn through the stitch by closing the latch and allowing the previous stitch to slip over the hook and yarn.

This makes a chain stitch. Hook the next stitch off the adjacent needle and pull through the chain stitch already on the latch tool, now work another chain stitch.

Repeat this sequence to the last stitch which is then fastened off as before with a knot.

PRACTICE: KNITTING A SNOOD

Practice these methods of casting on and off, knitting pieces 20 to 30 stitches wide and 20 rows long. Once you have mastered these techniques, try knitting a 'snood'. This is a tubular head scarf which can also be worn as a loose collar.

SNOOD

INSTRUCTIONS FOR A STANDARD GAUGE MACHINE

Use a 4 ply acrylic yarn. Approx 100 g. MT approx 6 to 8.

Method

Cast on 160 sts with a closed edge (either 'e-wrap' or latch tool). Set RC to 000. Knit 250 rows.
Cast off loosely.

INSTRUCTIONS FOR A CHUNKY MACHINE

Use DK acrylic yarn. Approx 150 g. MT approx 4 to 5.

Method

Cast on 100 sts with a closed edge (either 'e-wrap' or latch tool). Set RC to 000. Knit 120 rows.
Cast off loosely.

Making up (both versions)

Tack the long sides together and try for size. If the finished snood is too tight or too long, re-knit using more stitches and fewer rows. If it is too wide and short, then knit again with fewer stitches and more rows. Once you are satisfied that the size is correct, sew the seams. Do not press the fabric but allow the ends to roll.

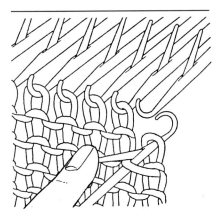

Latch tool cast off (from RHS).

Snoods are easy to make and fun to wear (pp. 30–31).

INCREASING AND DECREASING

In machine knitting most of the shaping is worked at the ends of the row. It is possible to increase (Inc) or decrease (Dec) along the row by knitting several rows in waste yarn and then taking the knitting off the machine, the work is replaced on to the needles, increasing or decreasing to the required number of stitches. The waste yarn is removed and the knitting continued. This technique, however, is not often used, it is easier to shape by changing the stitch size rather than by increasing or decreasing stitches across the row.

TIPS

□ *When increasing or decreasing the stitches are transferred before the row is knitted. So, when reading a pattern, the instruction 'increase (or decrease) 1 st each end of the next and following 4th row' means that you must increase (or decrease) by moving 1 needle, or stitch, each end of the knitting, then move the carriage across the needles, then back, then across and back again, so knitting 4 rows. Then increase (or decrease) 1 st each end again and knit the row. It will help the increased, or decreased, stitches to knit correctly if you push the needles carrying the new stitches forward to HP, knit across.*
□ *Where machines have no Hold setting, such as the Bond and Knitmaster Zippy 90, push the needles to the UWP so that the stitches are behind the open latches; these will then knit back correctly.*

INCREASING

SIMPLE INCREASE

Used to increase one stitch at a time. The edge produced by this method is rather loose with large looped stitches. This is the easiest way to increase.

Method
Push one empty needle forward at either end of the working needles, either to WP, UWP, or HP. These will knit back and stitches will be formed as the knitting continues.

The school jumper, shown with the boy's jumper which uses the roundneck shape with Fair Isle decoration (stitch pattern Toyota 901 card 8).

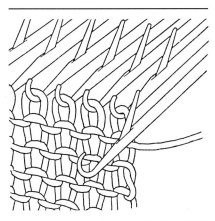

Simple increase: *push one needle from NWP to WP, UWP, or HP.*

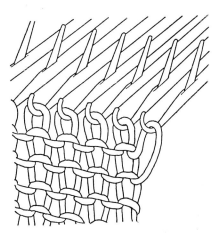

Simple increase: *knit one row. The empty needle picks up the yarn.*

FULLY FASHIONED INCREASE

This produces a neater, firmer edge. The new stitch is formed several stitches in from the edge as the existing end stitches are moved outwards.

Method (diagrams p. 40)
Use the single pronged transfer tool and transfer the end stitch on to the next empty needle which is brought from NWP. The needle from which the stitch was taken is left in WP. A new stitch is formed on the needle when the carriage is moved across the bed, making a hole.
The hole can be avoided by picking up the heel of the adjacent stitch and placing it on the empty needle.
The fully fashioned technique is also worked by moving 2 or more stitches outwards using either the 2 or 3-pronged transfer tools, but only one new stitch is made at a time.
Remember one stitch can be increased at each end of a row, so that the total number of stitches is increased by 2.

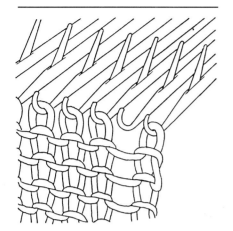

Fully fashioned increase: *one stitch moved out one needle.*

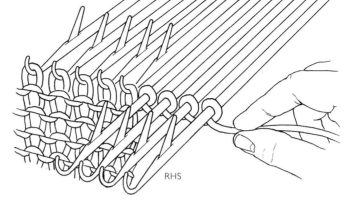

Multiple increase using the 'e-wrap' cast on; carriage at RHS.

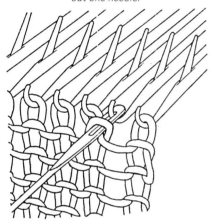

Fully fashioned increase: *put the heel of adjacent stitch onto empty needle.*

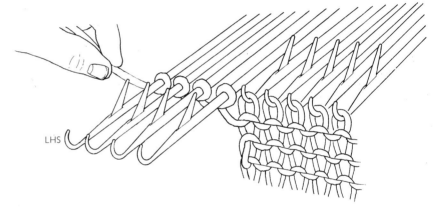

Multiple increase using 'e-wrap' cast-on; carriage at LHS.

MULTIPLE INCREASE

This method is used to increase a number of stitches at the beginning of a row. It is worked at the end of the row nearest to the carriage. In order to make a symmetrical shape (if required) the second increase is worked at the beginning of the next row.

Method

Use the 'e-wrap' method. Cast on over the required number of extra needles in HP at the end nearest the carriage. Check that the yarn has not caught on the sinker plate assembly, then knit across.
Bring forward to HP the required needles at the opposite end of the work and 'e-wrap' over these needles, then knit as in previous row.
It will help the new stitches to knit correctly if the needles are pushed to HP (or UWP) for 6 to 8 rows and the claw weights hung at the cast-on edge of the new stitches as soon as practicable. If further multiple increases are made, re-hang the weights.

DECREASING

Where gradual shaping is required 1 or 2 stitches are reduced at a time by using the transfer tool. This can be done at both ends of the same row. Where 3 or more stitches are decreased, the stitches are cast off, making a step at the edge of the knitting. (For this method the instruction will normally say, for example, 'Cast off 3 stitches at the beginning of the next row'.)

SIMPLE DECREASE

Transfer the first stitch at each end of the knitting to the adjacent needle carrying a stitch. Push the empty needles back to NWP. The two stitches will be knitted together on one needle when the carriage is moved across.

TIP
☐ *If the pattern instructions ask for one stitch to be decreased at each end of every alternate row, try decreasing 2 stitches at each end of every 4th row*

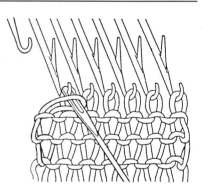

Simple decrease: *transfer end stitch to adjacent needle using single transfer tool.*

using the 2-pronged transfer tool. This will achieve the same result and is quicker to knit.

FULLY FASHIONED DECREASE

This gives a neat edge with an attractive line of shaping.

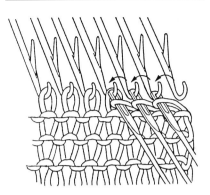

Fully fashioned decrease using 3 pronged transfer tool. Move stitches one needle inwards.

Method

Using the 3-pronged transfer tool, transfer the 3 end stitches 1 needle inwards. Move the empty needle back to NWP. The 3rd needle in from the end will now hold 2 stitches which are knitted together as the carriage is moved across.

A more obvious line of decreasing can be made by moving 5 stitches at a time. Use the 2-pronged transfer tool and transfer the stitches from the 4th and 5th needles on to the 5th and 6th needles. Then take the 3-pronged transfer tool and transfer the stitches from the 1st, 2nd and 3rd needles to the 2nd, 3rd and 4th needles. Push the empty needle back to NWP. There will now be 2 stitches on the 5th needle from the end.

Another variation is to decrease 2 stitches at a time. To do this use the 2-pronged transfer tool to transfer the stitches on the 4th and 5th needles to the 6th and 7th needles then use the 3 pronged tool to transfer the stitches on the 1st, 2nd and 3rd needles to the 3rd, 4th and 5th needles. Push the 2 empty needles back to NWP and continue to knit.

TIP
☐ *To prevent the decreasing from pulling tight, hang the claw weights at each edge. Move the weights up as you knit. This is particularly important when shaping raglan sleeves or on the first side of a V-neck.*

MULTIPLE DECREASE

This is another term for casting off.

RIBS, MOCK RIBS AND HEMS

Used when a firmer band of knitting with a finished edge is required for the welts, cuffs and neckband of a garment. Mock ribs and hems have two layers of fabric, ribs a single layer.

Mock Ribs:
These ribs look similar to a true rib (see below) and are easily knitted on a single bed machine. Needles left out of work cause gaps which create the appearance of purl stitches. (Mock ribs are known as 'ribbed hems' because there are two layers of fabric.)

Hems:
No needles are left out of work so there is no rib effect, and a plain stocking stitch hem is formed. The 'cast on' open edge is picked up and knitted with the last row of the hem so that the hem is completed before the main body of knitting is worked, unlike sewing when the hem is worked on finishing the garment. Decorative 'picot' edges can be worked on hems. Neckbands and borders are worked in the same way as hems and can either be knitted or sewn down to finish the garment.

Ribs, mock ribs and hems are usually worked in a smaller stitch size than the main knitting as this gives a firmer section of knitting for the edge of a garment.

Ribs:
A rib is a stitch pattern formed by alternately knitting and purling stitches in the same row. It is possible to make such a pattern using a single bed machine but the necessary stitches have to be 'turned round' manually using the latch tool.

MOCK RIBS

1 x 1 HEM (MOCK RIB)
A 1 x 1 hem gives a rib-like appearance producing a hem with some elasticity. It uses waste yarn, nylon cord, main yarn and the single-pronged transfer tool.

TIPS
☐ *Use waste yarn and main yarn in contrasting colours. This way it is easier to see which is the waste yarn.*
☐ *The instruction 'Cast on for 1 x 1 mock rib over 31 needles' means: Push*

31 needles to WP, 16 on LHS and 15 on RHS of the centre 0 on the needle bed. Then using the 1 x 1 needle pusher return every alternate needle to NWP. So there will be 16 needles left in WP and the mock rib will be worked over these needles only.

Method: Knitting hem (mock rib)
Bring to WP the required number of needles.
Arrange the needles so that every alternate needle is in WP.
Cast on using waste yarn (an open edge or woven method that is easy on your machine).
Work 6 to 8 rows. Break waste yarn.
Knit 1 row with nylon cord. Do this by threading the nylon cord into the carriage securing the end under the machine.
Hold the long free end of the cord above the carriage as though it was coming down from the tension arm and slightly towards the back of the machine.
With the other hand move the carriage across allowing the nylon cord to knit in, control the tension by allowing the cord to be drawn into the carriage and knitted.
At the end of the row remove the cord from the carriage.
Thread MY (main yarn) into the carriage, securing the free end under the machine.
Set the stitch size to MT − 2, RC 000.
Knit the required number of rows to make the finished depth of hem, for example, 10 rows.
Knit a turning row of large sized stitches at MT + 2. This makes a line of stitches which will form the fold line. Restore the tension dial to the setting of the first 10 rows, i.e., MT − 2, and knit a further 10 rows. (The RC will now read 021.)

The hem is now completed by folding it in half and knitting up the first row. To do this look at the knitting that has been worked so far. (See diag. p. 43.)
The sequence from the start is − waste yarn, nylon cord and main yarn, with a loose row of knitting across the middle. Fold the knitting at the loose row, this brings the nylon cord row up to the level of the needles.

Method: Joining hem (mock rib)
Hold the knitting at the fold, allow the waste yarn to fold back exposing the nylon cord.
To join the hem use the single-pronged transfer tool to pick up the loops of MY which lie between the nylon cord loops. Place the MY loops on to the empty needles that were in NWP   *cont.*

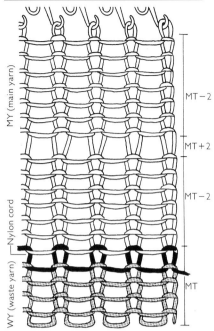

Knitting before joining a l × l rib showing WY and nylon cord.

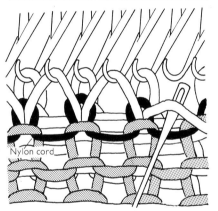

Pick up loops between nylon cord, using a single pronged transfer tool.

When all the loops are picked up every needle will be in WP.

Work I row on MT + I to make a joining row which is not too tight, so avoiding the hem sticking out.

Set the tension dial to the MT and the RC to 000. Knit a few rows, then break the yarn and take the knitting from the machine. You will, at this point, have a rather loose-looking hem.

Remove the waste yarn by pulling out the nylon cord. Take a straight edge (a ruler for example) and slide it between

Opposite: *Mock rib and hem samples. (From top) I × I mock rib, 2 × I mock rib, 3 × I mock rib, hem, hem with picot edge, latched rib.*

the two layers of knitting. Hold the top section of knitting and pull the straight edge down. The resulting pulled hem has a rib-like appearance and can be lightly steamed if the yarn is wool or will set when washed if the yarn is acrylic.

2 × I HEM (MOCK RIB)

This is used to give a softer 'rib' than the I × I hem. The needle arrangement is made by putting the required number of needles into WP then pushing back to NWP every third needle. The mock rib is knitted in the same way as the I × I hem up to the joining row. Cast on with waste yarn and knit a few rows, then knit I row with the nylon cord. Use MY (MT − 2) and knit the 2 sides of the hem with the loose row in the middle.

Now fold along the loose stitch row. You will see that the MY loops between the nylon cord are of different lengths − long and short.

Pick up the first loop and place it on the first needle, which already carries a stitch.

The second longer loop is put on to the empty third needle. The next short loop is put on to either of the next 2 needles carrying stitches, and so on down the row, always placing the long loops on to empty needles.

If a line of holes is required at the top of the hem, then put all the MY loops, between the nylon cord loops, on to the needles already carrying stitches and bring the empty needles to WP before knitting the joining row. The hem is completed as given in the I × I hem.

3 × I HEM (MOCK RIB)

Another rib-like effect is achieved by setting 3 needles in WP and I needle in

NWP. The same rules are observed as for the 2 × I hem when picking up the first row of MY knitting.

HEMS

These give an alternative finish to the mock rib for welts, neck and button bands.

Method

The process of making a hem is the same as that for mock ribs except that every needle is used. When turning up the hem, all the MY loops between the nylon cord loops on the first row of MY knitting are picked up and put on the needles, which are already carrying stitches. There will always be one loop less than the number of stitches. To make a neat edge the last loop is put on to the last needle carrying a stitch, missing out the second to last needle. The joining row must be knitted loosely.

PICOT EDGE

This is a hem with a decorative edge.

Method

Cast on over all the needles required. Use waste yarn and knit 6 to 8 rows. Knit I row with nylon cord and then knit the number of rows required up to the row before the fold row. In order to give a more pronounced 'picot' edge this row is worked in a larger stitch size, MT + 2. Before working the next row use the single pronged transfer tool to transfer every alternate stitch to the adjacent needle. Leave the empty needles in WP. Knit one row at MT + 2.

Reset the tension dial to the hem stitch size and knit the second side of *cont.*

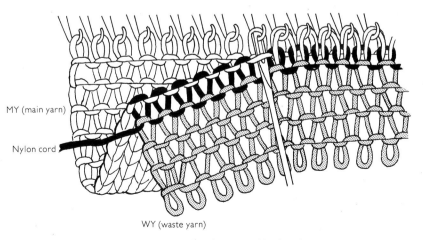

Hems: pick up every loop in Ist row MY for a hem.

the hem. Turn up hem as given for a plain hem.

TIP
□ *If you have a machine which has a separate lace carriage and which selects the needles to UWP when patterning (Brother and Toyota), then you can transfer the stitches for the picot edge with the lace carriage. Push the needles carrying stitches to be transferred to the UWP. Put the lace carriage on the bed at the opposite end to the main carriage and move it across. The selected stitches will be transferred. All the needles will be in UWP so push them back to WP and then continue knitting.*

NEEDLE POSITIONS WHEN KNITTING HEMS

The number of needles required when knitting a mock rib or hem can be adjusted to give a balanced needle setting.
For example: On a 1 x 1 hem, if an even number of stitches is required for the main knitting then work the hem using 1 stitch fewer or 1 stitch more than required. Increase or decrease the extra stitch when the hem has been completed.
On a 2 x 1 hem, the needles are arranged
either
||–||–||–||–||–||–||–||
or
|–||–||–||–||–||–||–||–|
Again 1 more or 1 fewer needle can be brought into use for the hem then an increase or decrease made on completion.

RIBS

A true rib is a single thickness of fabric with an arrangement of knit and purl stitches worked across the row.

This type of rib can only be worked on a single bed machine by using the latch tool to transform either every other, or every third stitch. This is a time-consuming method, but very useful for ribs on baby garments on the standard gauge machine, or any garment on a chunky machine, where relatively few stitches are used.

Method

Push the full number of needles required to WP. Arrange the needles so that every alternate needle is returned to NWP except at each end where the last 2 needles should be left together in WP.
||–|–|–|–|–|–|–|–|–|–|–|–||

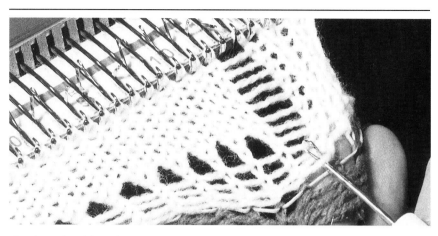
Latch up rib: *pick up the 1st loop of MY (light-coloured wool); then take the 3rd rung of the ladder through under the 1st loop. Note nylon cord.*

Cast on with waste yarn and knit 6 to 8 rows.
Knit 1 row with the nylon cord.
Push all the needles carrying stitches to HP. Take the main yarn and, starting at the opposite end to the carriage, 'e-wrap' across the needle bed. Thread the yarn into the carriage.
Knit 2 rows at MT – 2. Pick up the MY loop between the first and second needles at the opposite end to the carriage and place it on the first needle.
At the carriage end pick up the loop between the first and second needles and put it on to the second needle. Find the loop at the bottom of the first stitch and put it on the first needle.
Bring the needles from NWP to WP and knit the required number of rows.
The stitches to be 'knitted', that is turned from purl to plain, are now dropped from the needles one at a time and allowed to run down to form a ladder. The stitches dropped correspond to the needles that were originally in NWP.
Using the latch tool pick up the first loop of MY, miss 2 strands or bars of the ladder then pull the third bar through the first loop.

Continue knitting up the ladder of bars. At the top take the hook of the empty needle in the hook of the latch tool. Allow the stitch to slip back on to the needle. Work across the bed until all the selected stitches are knitted.

HAND KNITTED RIBS

It is possible to hand knit a rib and use it with machine knitting. The easiest way is to start the machine knitting on waste yarn, knit the main section and then unravel the waste yarn, picking up the MY stitches with knitting needles to knit the rib. A cast-off hand-knit rib edge can be tight so it helps if a larger size needle is used for casting off. You can save time by knitting the ribs after the main part of the garment is completed, because if you are not satisfied with the machine knitting part it is far quicker to re-knit this than the hand knitting. Another advantage of this method is that it is often difficult to stretch hand knit ribs sufficiently across the needles when trying to put them on to the machine.

PRACTICE – KNITTING A GLOVE PUPPET

This practice piece is designed as half of a glove puppet and covers making a hem, increasing and decreasing, and casting off.

The actual size knitted is unimportant. To make the puppet two identical pieces should be knitted. Two sizes are given, as a guide, to fit a large and a small hand.

Knit glove puppets – two sizes are given here – to practise making a hem, increasing and decreasing, casting off and sewing up. (See also p. 63).

GLOVE PUPPET

Knit two identical pieces.

Notes, abbreviations and suggestions

Dec: Decrease; use any method you like for practice in this piece
Inc: Increase; any chosen method
× 10: Inc/Dec 10 times in all
× 8: Inc/Dec 8 times in all
× 7: Inc/Dec 7 times in all
× 6: Inc/Dec 6 times in all
Casting off can be done by any method you choose.

ON A STANDARD GAUGE MACHINE

Use 4 ply acrylic yarn or equivalent. A stitch size (MT) of 6, 7 or 8 is suggested. Note that the figures in brackets refer to the small size, and the others to the larger size.

Method

Cast on for a 1 × 1 mock rib hem over 37 (29) needles.
Work a hem 14 rows deep as follows:
At MT − 2 cast on with WY, knit 6 to 8 rows, then knit 1 row with nylon cord.
Change to MY, at MT − 2 knit 14 rows, at MT + 2 knit 1 row, at MT − 2 knit 14 rows.
Turn up hem and knit joining row at MT + 2.
RC 000. MT. Knit 40 (26) rows.
RC 040. (026). Dec 1 st at each end of next and every alternate row × 10 (8). 17 (13) sts remain.
RC 059 (041). Knit 1 row.
RC 060 (042). MT + 2. Knit 1 row.
RC 061 (043). MT. Knit 1 row.
RC 062 (044). Inc 1 st each end on next and every alternate row × 10 (8). 37 (29) sts.
RC 083 (059). Knit 1 row. Cast off.

ON A CHUNKY MACHINE

Use a DK acrylic yarn or equivalent. A stitch size (MT) of 4 or 5 is suggested. Note that the figures in brackets refer to the small size, and the others to the larger size.

Method

Cast on for a 1 × 1 mock rib hem over 25 (21) needles.
Work a hem 8 rows deep as follows:
At MT − 2 cast on with WY, knit 6 to 8 rows, then knit 1 row with nylon cord.
Change to MY, at MT − 2 knit 8 rows, at MT + 2 knit 1 row, at MT − 2 knit 8 rows.
Turn up hem and knit joining row at MT + 2.
RC 000. MT. Knit 30 (20) rows.
RC 030 (020). Dec 1 st at each end of next and every alternate row × 7 (6). 11 (9) sts remain.
RC 045 (033). Knit 1 row.
RC 046 (034). MT + 2. Knit 1 row.
RC 047 (035). Knit 1 row.
RC 048 (036). Inc 1 st at each end on next and every alternate row × 7 (6). 25 (21) sts.
RC 061 (047). Knit 1 row. Cast off.

Making up

The instructions for making up the puppets and hints for decoration are given later in the section 'Making Up' on page 62.

TENSION

The techniques given in the previous sections provide sufficient knowledge of machine knitting to enable you to knit a jumper. There is, however, one very important point to consider before starting to knit and that is the TENSION. How many stitches and rows will be needed to make the garment? To establish this a sample, of at least 10 cm square, must be knitted and measured. A tension swatch can have any number of stitches or rows provided a known number of rows and stitches are measured. It is much easier to measure a known number of rows or stitches than to count the number of rows or stitches in a given measurement. The area measured should be marked in the centre of a piece of knitting, as the edge stitches are tight and the open ends at top and bottom stretch and unravel.

TENSION SWATCH

When using a pattern you will find a tension given, for example, 32 sts and 42 rows to a 10 cm square. Do not try to knit a 10 cm square by casting on 32 sts and working 42 rows. It will be difficult to measure accurately. Instead, knit a tension swatch of more stitches and rows than stated, marking a specified number of stitches and rows as you work.

STOCKING STITCH TENSION

To knit a stocking stitch tension swatch you will need your main yarn (MY) and a contrast yarn of the same or a similar thickness.

Method for standard gauge (or chunky) machine

Bring forward to WP 70 [36] needles arranged evenly over the central 0, i.e. LHS 35 + RHS 35 [LHS 18 + RHS 18]. Push back to NWP the 21st [11th] needle either side of 0.
Use the same stitch size throughout [MT].
Thread carriage with main yarn [MY] and secure end.
Cast on and knit 8 rows   *cont.*

Slash neck jumper (pp. 52–6) and Fair Isle slipover (pp. 92–3), both knitted in 4 ply.

Remove MY from carriage but do not break off.
Move the yarn clear of the carriage and hold it at the end of the bed.
Check your instruction book to see if there is a notch to hold the yarn on your machine.
Thread a contrast coloured yarn into the carriage and knit 2 rows.
Break and remove the contrast yarn. Re-thread MY.
Set RC to 000. Knit 60 [30] rows.
Remove MY from machine as before.
Thread in contrast yarn and knit 2 rows.
Break and remove yarn.
Re-thread MY and knit 8 rows. Break and remove yarn.
Release knitting from machine.

TIP
□ *To mark the stitch size used in the tension swatch work an equivalent number of stitches, either knitting by hand using a contrast yarn, or transferring stitches to adjacent needles to make holes. Make the marking several rows after the final 2 contrast coloured rows, then knit 5 or 6 rows before removing the knitting from the needles.*

TENSION SWATCH IN PATTERNED STITCH

The pattern swatch is knitted over the same number of needles as given above but the 21st [11th] needles are left in WP.

Method for standard gauge (or chunky) machine

The stitch pattern is knitted throughout and the same stitch size MT used throughout.
Put 70 [36] needles into WP.
Cast on. Knit 1 row.
Start to knit in pattern. Knit 8 rows.
Change to contrast coloured yarn. Knit 2 rows in pattern.

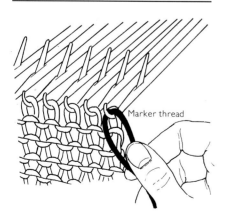

Positioning and holding a marker thread.

(Top) *Stocking stitch tension swatch knitted on a standard gauge machine, 'green' ruler measuring rows between contrast coloured rows.* **(Bottom)** *Patterned stitch tension swatch knitted on a Chunky machine, 'blue' ruler measuring stitches between marker threads.*

Re-thread MY. Set RC to 000. Knit 15 [5] rows.
Mark the 21st [11th] needle either side of 0 with a short length of contrasting yarn hung over the hook of each needle. Move the carriage across the bed, holding the marker threads clear of the carriage.
Repeat the marking at RC 030 [012] and RC 045 [020].
Knit to RC 060 [030]. Remove MY from carriage and change to contrast yarn. Knit 2 rows.
Re-thread MY and finish with several more rows [6 to 8].

MEASURING A SWATCH

When the swatch is taken off the machine it should be left for at least 2 hours before it is measured. This allows the stitches to relax into shape. It is im-portant to treat the tension swatch in the same way that the finished garment will be treated. For example, natural fibres may shrink, stretch or change shape when washed. Some man-made fibres alter when pressed. These treatments must be applied to the swatch before it is measured.

For the measuring itself use a tape measure or ruler. Place the swatch on to a flat non-slippery surface without stretching it. Measure the stitches between the inner edges of the ladders of the stocking stitch swatch and between the markers of the pattern stitch swatch. The rows are then measured between the top and bottom of the stitches of the contrast coloured rows.

Take the average of the 3 measurements having measured to one place of decimals; for example 14.3 cm, 14.4 cm and 14.3 cm gives an average 14.3 cm.

Keep a record of the measurements. When working out your own garment patterns, you will need to know how many stitches and rows there are needed to make 10 cm. With the help of a pocket calculator this is very easy to work out.

CALCULATING STITCHES TO 10 cm

Enter the number of stitches measured, then press the ÷ button. Enter the measured length of the stitches and then the = button.

Example: Number of stitches 40
Divide by width of 40sts, e.g.
14.3 cm
$40 ÷ 14.3 = 2.79$ sts per cm

To find how many stitches in 10 cm multiply (×) by 10 giving 27.9 stitches in 10 cm. As you cannot knit .9 of a stitch, make the number of stitches in 10 cm up to 28.

CALCULATING ROWS TO 10 cm

The method of calculating the number of rows in 10 cm is the same as that for stitches.

Example: 60 rows measure 14.9 cm
$60 ÷ 14.9$ cm $= 4.02$ rows in 1 cm.

So in 10 cm there will be 40 rows.

CALCULATING THE TENSION

The formula for calculating the tension of your knitting is:

The number of rows or stitches divided by the measured length of that number of rows or stitches. This gives the number of rows or stitches in 1 cm and is multiplied by 10 to give the number of rows or stitches in 10 cm.

(10 cm is equivalent to 4 in.)

TIP
□ *This formula can be used when measuring over any known number of stitches or rows. It is sometimes necessary and helpful to knit a tension swatch over more stitches and rows than 40[20] and 60[30] particularly if a stitch pattern like tuck, slip or lace is used.*

'GREEN' and 'BLUE' RULERS

These are rulers produced by Knitmaster primarily designed for use with the Knit Radar, a charting device which enables the knitter to follow a half-size scale diagram of the garment as it is knitted. The green ruler is used to measure knitting from a standard gauge machine over 40 sts and 60 rows. The blue ruler is used to measure knitting from a chunky machine over 20 sts and 30 rows. The readings give the number of stitches or rows in 10 cm. (The rulers can be used by users of any knitting machine, but other makes of charting device use measurements in centimetres not converted into the ratio of stitches or rows per 10 cm)

TIPS
Matching tension to written pattern instructions.
□ *If you have too many stitches or rows in 10 cm try a larger stitch size. If you have too few stitches or rows try a smaller stitch size.*
□ *Increasing the stitch size setting on the tension dial may reduce the number of stitches but not change the number of rows in 10 cm.*
□ *Remember the stitch size can be altered by using the 'dots' between the whole numbers on the Tension Dial.*
□ *The tension discs on the yarn tension mast can also be adjusted to alter the stitch size.*
□ *If you can obtain the required number of stitches in 10 cm but not the required number of rows then use that stitch size to knit the garment but adjust the number of rows.*

It is important to knit a tension swatch before knitting a garment because otherwise you may have to re-knit the whole garment. It is much easier to check a small swatch of knitting first.

With practice you will find it easier to work out a garment pattern using your own tension than to try to match a tension given in a written pattern.

PATTERN STITCHES AND GARMENTS

PLAIN STOCKING STITCH

The first garment to knit is a simple slash necked sweater pattern, given in three sizes for either standard gauge or chunky machines. A second set of instructions offering knitters the opportunity to work out their own pattern with hints, guidance, and a measurement chart are included in a later section.

Subsequent garment patterns cover a different construction technique and stitch pattern. The first jumper is very simple with two identical pieces for the back and front, and shaped sleeves.

SLASH NECK JUMPER

CHUNKY MACHINE

Size: To fit 34(36,38) in/85(90,95) cm bust/chest.
Yarn: 600 g Aran thickness wool and acrylic. (No pressing needed.)
Tension: 16.5 stitches and 25 rows to a 10 cm square.

Front and back

Knit 2 pieces alike.
Cast on with waste yarn for 1 x 1 latched rib over 82(87,90) sts. Knit 6–8 rows.
Knit 1 row with nylon cord.
Thread MY, work 'e-wrap' cast on, then knit 2 rows at MT−2.
Pick up loops of end stitches on first row and place on to end needles.
Bring remaining empty needles to WP. Knit 14 rows.
Drop stitches from needles originally in NWP and latch them up missing out the 2nd and 3rd bars and working 1 stitch at a time.
RC 000. MT. Knit to RC 068(076,078). Mark the end stitches with a short length of contrast yarn.

TIP

□ *Do not knit the stitches with contrast yarn as this would cause a dropped stitch when the yarn is removed, but lay the contrast yarn in the hook of the needle and hold the ends down clear of the carriage for the first row.*

Continue knitting to RC 125(136,140)

Neckband

Arrange needles for 2 x 1 mock rib by transferring every 3rd stitch to the adjacent needle. Knit 1 row MT, 7 rows MT−2, 1 row MT+1, 7 rows MT−2, 1 row MT.
Take the main yarn from the yarn feeder and leave a long end approximately 3 times the length of the knitting.
Finish with 6–8 rows of waste yarn and

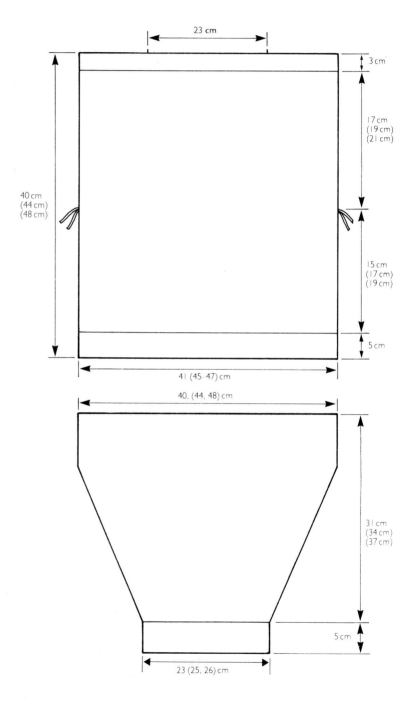

Child's Slash Neck Jumper:
Sizes 28 (30, 32) in chest/Sizes 70 (75, 80) cm chest

remove knitting from the machine.
Use the length of MY to sew down the
neckband slipstitching through each
stitch, one by one, to purl side of the
knitting.

Sleeves

Knit 2 alike.
Cast on with waste yarn for 1 × 1 mock
rib over 44(47,50) sts.

Knit 6–8 rows then 1 row with nylon
cord.
With MY, knit cuff as follows: 14 rows
MT − 2, 1 row MT + 1, 14 rows MT − 2.
Pick up loops of first row of MY knit-
ting and place them on empty needles.
Push all needles to WP, then knit 1 row
MT + 1.
RC 000. MT. Knit 10 rows.
RC 010. Inc 1 st each end of next and

every following 4th row × 21 times
in all.
RC 090. Knit without further shaping
to RC 100(108,116). Cast of loosely.

Making up

Join neckband at shoulder, leaving
23 cm in the centre for the neck opening. Sew in sleeves between the markers on back and front. Sew side and
sleeve seams. Sew cuffs in 2 separate
layers using matress stitch. (See 'Making-up a Garment' pp. 58–64.)

STANDARD GAUGE MACHINE

Size: To fit 28(30,32) in/70(75,80) cm
bust/chest.
Yarn: 250 g 4 ply acrylic (no pressing)
Tension: 28 stitches and 39 rows to a
10 cm square.

Front and back

Knit 2 pieces alike.
Cast on with waste yarn for 1 × 1 mock
rib over 114(126,132) needles. Knit 6–8
rows.
Knit 1 row with nylon chord.
Thread MY. MT − 2 knit 14 rows.
MT + 2 knit 1 row. MT − 2 knit 14 rows.
Pick up loops and place on empty
needles. Knit 1 row MT + 1.
RC 000. MT. Knit straight to RC
060(066,074).
Mark the end stitches with a short
length of contrast yarn.

TIP
□ *Do not knit stitches with the contrast
yarn as this would cause a dropped
stitch when the yarn is removed. Lay
the contrast yarn in the hook of the
needle and hold the ends down clear of
the carriage for the first row.*

Continue knitting to RC 126(140,156).

Neckband

Arrange needles for 2 × 1 mock rib by
transferring every 3rd stitch to the adjacent needle.
Knit 1 row MT, 7 rows MT − 2, 1 row
MT + 1, 7 rows MT − 2, 1 row MT. Take
the MY from the feeder and leave a long
end of yarn approximately 3 times the
length of the knitting.
Finish with 6 to 8 rows in waste yarn
and remove knitting from the machine.
Use the length of MY to sew down the
neckband, slipstitching through each
stitch, one by one, to the purl side of
the knitting.

Sleeves

Knit 2 alike.
Cast on with waste yarn for a 1 × 1 *cont.*

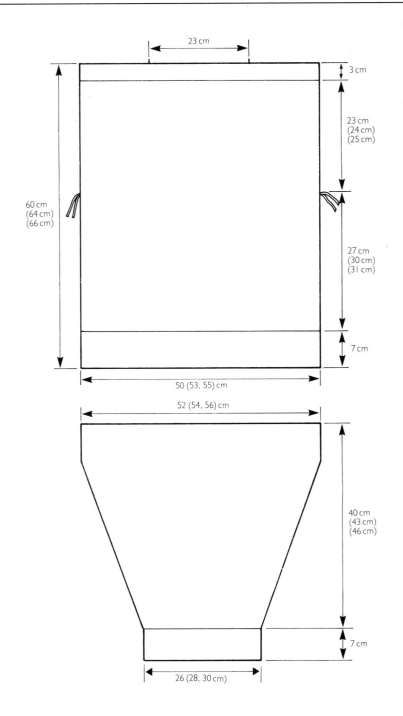

Adult's Slash Neck Jumper:
Sizes 34 (36, 38) in chest/Sizes 85 (90, 95) cm chest

mock rib over 64(70,74) sts.
Knit 6–8 rows. Knit 1 row with nylon cord.
Work mock rib in MY as given for front and back.
RC 000. MT. Knit 10 rows straight.

Opposite: *Slash neck jumper knitted in a fancy yarn, here a bouclé.*

Inc 1 st each end of next and every following 4th row × 24(26,30).
112(122,134) sts.
Work straight to RC 120(132,144).
Cast off.

Making up

Join shoulder seams leaving 23 cm open at centre for neck opening. Sew in sleeves between markers on back and front. Sew side and underarm seams. Sew mock ribs in two layers using matress stitch. (See 'Making-up a Garment' on pp. 58–64.)

ADAPTING THE SLASH NECK JUMPER

The slash neck jumper can be adapted to your own measurements and to

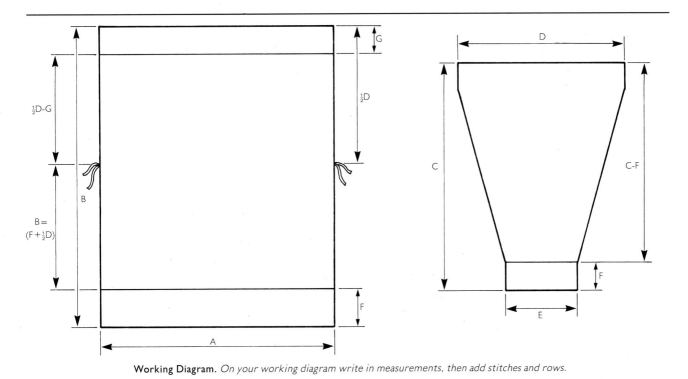

Working Diagram. *On your working diagram write in measurements, then add stitches and rows.*

MEASUREMENTS FOR SLASH-NECK JUMPER

Actual chest/bust in inches	18	20	22	24	26	28	30	32	34	36	38	40	42	44	46	
Actual chest/bust in cm	45	50	55	60	65	70	75	80	85	90	95	100	105	110	115	
KNITTED MEASUREMENTS IN CENTIMETRES (ease and extra length included)																
Front/back width	25	28	31	34	37	41	45	47	50	53	55	58	62	65	68	A
Back length	20	26	32	36	40	44	48	54	58	62	64	66	67	68	70	*B
Sleeve length	14	21	26	30	34	36	40	42	45	48	51	53	54	56	58	C
Top sleeve width	22	24	28	32	36	40	44	48	52	54	56	58	60	62	64	D
Wrist	10	12	14	15	17	18	19	20	22	24	24	25	25	26	27	E
Hems and cuffs**	3	3	3	4	4	4	5	5	5	7	7	7	7	7	7	F
Neck band***	2	2	2	2	2	2	3	3	3	3	3	4	4	4	4	G

* alter as required
** subtract this measurement from back and sleeve length
*** subtract this measurement from back length

different yarns. First measure chest to find the size needed. All the body measurements are given in centimetres. The chest/bust sizes are given in inches only as a size guide. The pattern measurement chart given for the slash neck jumper has 'ease' added.

Ease is the extra length or width added to body measurements to enable the wearer of a garment to be comfortable, to move without straining the knitting and to give fashion style to the garment.

Having selected the size, next check the back length. Measure from the bone at the base of the neck to the waist, and add extra length or shorten as required to suit the wearer.

For example, the 36 in chest size has about 18 cm added to the back length measurement. If the garment is to finish at the waist, then it is still necessary to add at least 5 cm for ease to the measured back length (back neck to waist), allowing for movement.

Method

1. Choose yarn and select stitch size.
2. Knit and measure tension swatch.
3. Pencil in measurements on working diagram. (See p. 55.)

TIP
□ *If you are knitting your first jumper then start with one for a child and knit it a size larger than actually needed. Then if the finished jumper is larger than expected, the child will grow into it, but if it is smaller than intended it should still fit.*

4. Calculate the number of rows and stitches to 1 cm.
5. Work out and write in the number of rows and stitches required to knit the back and front.

TIP
□ *A very rough guide for knitting welts and hems:*
For 1 × 1 four ply acrylic at MT − 2 work 5 rows per cm
For 2 × 1 four ply acrylic at MT − 2 work 4 rows per cm
For 1 × 1 Aran at MT − 2 work 2.5 rows per cm
For 2 × 1 Aran at MT − 2 work 2 rows per cm

The correct procedure would be to knit a tension swatch for the welts as well as the main fabric, so if you feel unsure do so, as the above is only a very rough guide.

CALCULATING STITCHES AND ROWS

To calculate stitches and rows needed to shape the sleeve:

1. Calculate the number of stitches needed at the cuff and at the top of the sleeve.
Example: Tension 2.8 sts to 1 cm

Top sleeve width:	52 cm
Sts needed:	52 × 2.8
	= 146
Cuff:	28 cm
Sts needed:	28 × 2.8
	= 78

(Numbers are rounded to nearest whole numbers.)

2. Calculate the difference in the number of stitches between the cuff and the sleeve top.
In the example 146 − 78 = 68 sts.
3. The increases are worked at each end of the row. The number of increases to be worked is found by dividing the difference in the number of stitches by 2. In the example 68 sts ÷ 2 = 34 increases.
4. Calculate the number of rows needed for the sleeve length.
Example: Tension 4 rows to 1 cm.
Length required 42 cm.
Number of rows: 4 × 42 = 168.
5. Share the number of increases evenly over the number of rows by dividing the number of rows by the number of increases.
Example: 168 ÷ 34 = 4.9 rows between increases.
6. Take the resulting number and if it is not a whole number forget the figure after the decimal point. In the example you would increase 1 st at each end on every 4th row. The extra rows needed to give the correct length are knitted straight when the shaping is finished.

TIP
□ *The sleeve is usually knitted from the cuff up to the shoulder as calculated above, but can also be knitted from the shoulder down to the cuff. This is done by decreasing instead of increasing. Before knitting, you must calculate the number of rows to be knitted before starting to decrease. The calculations are the same as in the cuff to shoulder method with the addition of calculating how many rows will be worked while shaping. This is done by multiplying the number of rows between decreases and the number of decreases worked. Example: rows between decreases = 4, number of decreases = 34. So total rows worked while shaping is 4 × 34 = 136. This figure is then subtracted from the total number of rows needed to give the correct length. Example: 168 rows total length − 136 rows shaping = 32 rows to be knitted before shaping.*

KNITTING THE SLASH NECK JUMPER

Back and front
Knit both alike.
Cast on for 1 × 1 welt over calculated number of sts.
Knit hem and turn up.
RC 000. MT. Knit to the row required to give length, B − (F + ½D).
Mark each end of row with waste yarn.
RC 000. Knit length ½D − G.

Neck band
Transfer every 3rd st to the adjacent needle to form a 2 × 1 mock rib.
Knit 1 row MT, then the number of rows for band depth at MT − 2. Work turning row at MT + 2, then work rows for band depth at MT − 2. Finally work 1 row at MT.
The band can be finished with waste yarn and sewn down later or you can pick up the long bars made where the first row of the band started (only the bars − this will be sufficient to hold the edge down). Cast off loosely.

Tip
□ *After knitting the back, leave for at least two hours then measure. If the results are satisfactory knit the rest of the garment. If not, undo, re-wind and start again. One of the advantages of machine knitting is the speed with which you can knit or re-knit a section of garment.*

Sleeves
Work either method 1 or 2.
1. Knitted from cuff upwards:
Work 1 × 1 hem and shape as calculated. Cast off or finish in waste yarn. Attach to back and front by sewing or knitting after joining shoulders.
2. Knitted from shoulder downwards: Join shoulders of back and front, leaving about 23 cm open for neck.
Along armhole edge, between markers, pick up the calculated number of stitches.
Knit and shape as calculated, working a 1 × 1 hem for the cuff.

This can either be finished with waste yarn and sewn down to finish or it can be picked up as on the neck band, picking up the long bars only and then casting off loosely.

Making up
Sew side and underarm seams.

The first time, try knitting the garment in stocking stitch, using an easy yarn in one colour only. Then experiment. Try knitting stripes, fancy yarns, etc. It is such a simple shape that it is ideal to practice with.

COMMON PROBLEMS IN PLAIN KNITTING

PROBLEM	CAUSE	REMEDY
Carriage jams	1. Carriage not set correctly on bed	Remove and replace carriage
	2. Cast on too tight, e.g. 'e-wrap'	Re-cast on
	3. Yarn tension too tight	Release yarn tension
	4. Yarn caught in tension arm	Check threading
	5. Yarn caught under carriage	Release and re-thread
	6. Knot in yarn	Pull knot clear
	7. Bent needles	Replace bent needles
Not knitting	1. Carriage set to slip	Re-set to knit
	2. Carriage set to hold	Reposition needles and re-set to knit
	3. Carriage not moved far enough past end needles	Take carriage back to yarn side and re-knit. Carriage should pass at least 5–7 cm from the needles in work on each row
Stitches all drop off (Usually quicker to start again)	1. Carriage not properly threaded	Re-thread and check
	2. Sinker plate assembly not attached properly	Check sinker plate screws and position
	3. Incorrect needle setting	Check needle setting
Stitches drop at start of row	1. Yarn incorrectly threaded	Check threading
	2. Yarn tension too loose	Tighten tension
	3. Yarn 'looped' under carriage	Check brushes run freely – if not unscrew, clean and replace
Stitches drop next to needles in hold	1. Stitch size too small as knitting is pushing up	Hang claw weights
	2. Yarn is not wrapped round next needle	Make sure that yarn is held under first needle in HP next to working needles
Stitches dropped mid row	1. Sinker plate assembly incorrectly fitted	Re-fit sinker plate assembly
	2. Yarn not properly threaded	Check threading
Stitches tucking	1. Stitch size too small	Undo and re-knit using larger stitch size
	2. Yarn too tight	Release yarn tension, check threading
	3. Stitches caught on sinker posts	Remove from sinker posts – see below
Stitches caught on sinker post	1. Fabric accidentally lifted over sinker posts – this is possible when checking stitches or when unravelling rows	Push needles round the caught area to UWP and gently push the fabric up from underneath and off the sinker posts. Return needles to UWP (or HP) Check no further loops caught
One stitch repeatedly tucking	1. Damaged needle – stitch not knitting off correctly	Change needle, see manual for method
Carriage stiff and dragging	1. Carriage not correctly placed on bed	Check position of carriage
	2. Sinker plate assembly not correctly fixed and/or bent	Check sinker plate assembly
	3. Lack of oil	Read manual, clean and oil

CORRECTING OTHER PROBLEMS

TOO MANY ROWS KNITTED

I. Put all needles carrying stitches to WP.
2. Pull yarn so that needles move forward slightly. The stitches are flattened and the hooks lie between the sinker posts. Remove yarn from carriage.
3. Pull the yarn firmly upwards and slightly towards the back of the machine, 'ripping' the yarn from the needles. Pull the yarn clear across the row.
4. Put all needles back to WP.
5. Pull yarn back through tension arm. Allow the yarn to pile on top of the cone. It is not necessary to rewind (except very slippery yarn). The yarn will knit back correctly from an undisturbed pile if you ensure that the yarn is not caught on any other yarn or on any part of the machine.
6. Repeat the unravelling for the excess number of rows.
7. If the carriage is at the opposite end to the yarn move the carriage back to the yarn side without knitting. To do this, set the carriage Part lever (Brother), Empty (Toyota) or Slip (Singer). Raise the carriage top (Knitmaster). Move the carriage across. (Needles not in WP and carrying stitches will move and drop the stitches.)
8. Reset the row counter by winding back the number of rows unpicked plus an extra row if the carriage was moved across without knitting.
9. Re-thread the yarn. Set the carriage to knit. Continue knitting.

(If knitting in pattern, see the notes on re-setting the pattern, p. 65.)

DROPPED STITCHES

To pick up one stitch which has been dropped and run down I or 2 rows, use the single pronged transfer tool. Insert it under the bar below the dropped stitch. It is much easier to pick up this stitch than the loop of the dropped stitch itself. Slip this picked up stitch back on to the needle hook, passing under the 'ladder'. Knit the stitch back up manually one 'rung' at a time.

When a long ladder occurs, the stitch is best picked up and worked with the latch tool up to the top of the ladder.

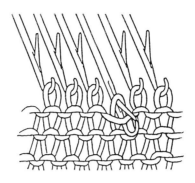

Dropped stitches:
manually knit back one row.

The latch tool is used through the back of the fabric. If used from the front a knit stitch, as in rib, would be made.

Method: Picking up dropped stitches

Catch the dropped stitch with either the pointed end of the crochet hook or the single pronged transfer tool.
Put the latch tool through the ladder from the knit to the purl side.
Take the stitch and latch up the rungs one at a time.
When the last rung is worked transfer the stitch to the single pronged transfer tool then back on to the needle hook.

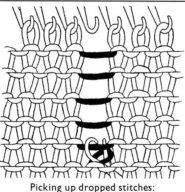

Picking up dropped stitches:
latch up from behind.

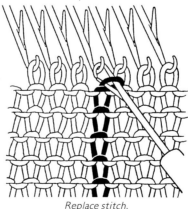

Replace stitch.

Alternative methods

Because it is difficult to get to the back of the fabric several methods are suggested.
I. Work up the ladder a few rungs at a time. The latch tool is held vertically, hook end down the ladder. The disadvantage is that the latch tool must be removed and replaced after working a few rungs.
2. Reach underneath the knitting and push the tool through the knitting almost horizontally. The fabric must be pulled taut as you work. This is awkward if there is a length of fabric to hold or a ribbing attachment in place.
3. The needles and stitches round the dropped stitch can be eased forward to UWP and HP. The latch tool can then pass down the gap produced and the stitch can be latched up. When the stitch is back on the hook the needles must be returned to WP very carefully.

TIP
□ Picking up dropped stitches is a time-consuming operation. Don't be afraid to take the work off the needles and start again – it may be quicker. If on completion of a garment you find I or 2 dropped stitches, these can be sewn down with matching thread. Even ladders can be crocheted up with the latch tool, then the last stitch secured in place. It is much easier to latch up stitches with the knit side facing you.

MAKING UP A GARMENT

BLOCKING AND PRESSING

These processes are applied to sections before the garment is sewn up.

BLOCKING

The garment pieces are pinned out to the required shape and measurements before they are pressed. Glass-headed pins are recommended as they are easier to use with knitted fabrics. The small heads of dressmaking pins can slip through the fabric. Plastic-headed pins should be avoided as they may melt, if

Opposite: *Simple lace stitch used to knit a sleeveless top based on the slash neck pattern finished with a picot edge (simple lace pattern taken from Sheet 10 No. 34 Brother 910 Electronic), and child's slash neck jumper decorated with stripes.*

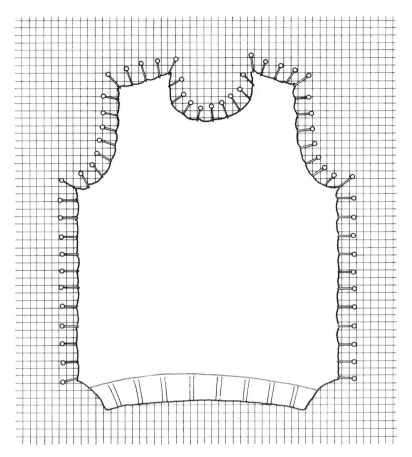

Making up: *how to block your knitting. Pin out to correct measurements.*

Sewing together: *slip stitch.*

2. To sew down stitches when turning up a hem or a border.

Method

When sewing down stitches of a mock rib border or hem, join on the thread. Work a small stitch in the main fabric first and then insert the needle up through the open stitch on the border then back down to the fabric again. This stitch can be worked loosely.

BACK STITCH

Uses

I. Where a strong seam is needed because there will be a strain on the fabric, for example, at armholes.
2. To give a neat finish to bands sewn down on the outside of the garment. *Note:* It can give a bulky seam.

pressed under a hot iron and spoil the fabric. Ribs are never pressed, this flattens the fabric and makes them less elastic.

TIP
□ *Where two identical pieces are to be pressed, block and press one piece first, then place the second piece over the first and pin and press again. This will ensure that both pieces are exactly the same size.*

PRESSING

Wool and natural fibres: Press with a hot iron after covering the knitting with a damp cloth.
Man-made fibres: Where the elasticity of the yarn is to be kept (for example with acrylic yarn to give a 'wool' look) do not press. If steaming equipment is available steam the fabric from underneath, i.e., apply no pressure but allow the steam to rise through the fabric. When a man-made fibre has been knitted with the intention of having a silky fabric the elasticity is purposely 'killed' by pressing and stretching the fabric when wet.

TIP
□ *Where knitted borders have been finished with waste yarn and are to be sewn in place, lightly press the last row of MY and the waste yarn. This sets the stitches and makes them easier to sew without them unravelling.*

SEWING SECTIONS TOGETHER

EQUIPMENT
Blunt ended tapestry needle, glassheaded pins, scissors, yarn which is either the main yarn of the garment, or a matching yarn which is thinner or without slubs.

SLIPSTITCH
It is not a strong stitch but is useful where the elasticity of the knitted fabric is to be retained, for example, on a round neck.

Uses
I. Where a flat join is required, for example to join the neckbands on the slash neck jumper.

Sewing together: *back stitch. Unravel* WY.

Method
When fastening off a length of thread, making running stitches over the last 3 or 4 cm, then turn and make running stitches back over the gaps in the first line, carrying on for a few stitches into the back stitch proper. Cut thread. When joining in a new length of thread, begin 3 or 4 cm after the required starting point and make running stitches back towards the start.
At the starting point turn and run back over the first running stitches. When these are covered start to back stitch normally.
This method of starting and finishing avoids bulky lumps in the seam.

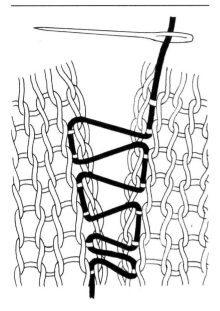

Sewing together: *mattress stitch.*

MATTRESS STITCH

Uses

1. Where a strong seam is required without bulk.
2. Particularly useful when matching patterns in knitting. It is worked from the bottom upwards with the right sides of both pieces facing. The stitches are made along a line of knitted stitches in such a way that the join is invisible.

To join two edges of a mock rib, or hem, use the MY and work from the joining row towards the fold. Start at the outside of the garment and mattress stitch the two outer layers together. When the fold line is reached, work back towards the joining row along the two inner layer edges. Keep the two layers, outer and inner, separate.

Method

After every few stitches, pull the thread gently to close the seam. Care is needed to avoid stitching back through the sewing thread, but it is easy to undo them when a mistake is made. Finish off the end of the thread down the inside of the seam.

GRAFTING OR KITCHENER STITCH

Use

Where two sections of knitting are joined together to give the appearance of a continuous piece of knitting. The knitted stitches are held on waste yarn which is unravelled as the sewing proceeds.

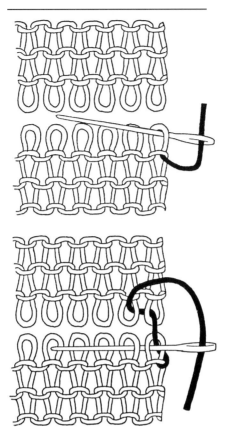

Sewing together: *grafting with knit side facing: (Top) Step 1. (Above) Step 2.*

Method

Care must be taken to make the sewn stitches the same size as those of the knitting. With practice this gives an invisible join. As the knitting is continuous without a seam line, shoulder 'seams' may stretch.

SWISS DARNING

Uses

1. Embroidery decoration.
2. To cover missed pattern stitches in Fair Isle.

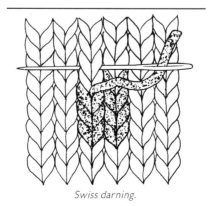

Swiss darning.

Method

Swiss darning is a very useful embroidery stitch if you need to introduce one small spot of colour, for example, the eye of an animal in a different colour from the motif and its background.

SEWING MACHINE

Knitted pieces can be successfully sewn together using a sewing machine. The sewing machine can also be used when knitted fabric has been cut to shape. Use a straight stitch where no stretch is needed and a strong seam is required, for example, side and sleeve seams, but a small swing stitch (zig-zag stitch size 1, stitch width 1) is usually recommended for sewing knitwear, particularly if the knitting has been cut, as this has some stretch.

Many manufacturers of sewing machines provide additional sewing feet for use with knitted fabrics. These have deep channels, rollers underneath, or the front end of the foot raised up to avoid catching the threads.

Brother make a binding wire. This is a long thin wire with a knob at one end which is used as a combination of pins and tacking thread. The edges to be sewn are 'tacked' with the binding wire, then either a zig-zag stitch over the wire or straight stitch along by the side can be used. The fabric being sewn needs to be eased along the wire as the sewing proceeds, this reduces stretching on the edges of the knitting. Always use a man-made sewing thread with knitting worked in man-made fibres or natural fibres if the knitting is not going to be pressed with a hot iron. Man-made thread has more elasticity than cotton.

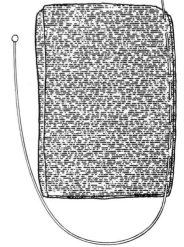

Sewing together on a sewing machine using a binding wire. NB: *The wire is straight in use.*

MAKING UP THE GLOVE PUPPET

Take the practice piece which was knitted following the instructions at the end of the section on Hems and Mock Ribs. (See p. 41.)
Knit another piece the same.
1. Sew the pieces together along the cast off edge with 'knit' sides together, using back stitch.
2. Fold the cast off edge down, along the fold line, with the 'purl' side out. Sew either side making a mouth.
3. Sew down the sides.
4. Join the welts in two separate layers.

The outer section can be back stitched and the inner section mattress stitched.
5. Finish off all remaining ends of yarn.
6. Decorate the face.

Suggestions: the eyes could be buttons or cross stitch; the nose could be satin stitch or made of felt or fabric; the mouth could be Swiss darned.

ALTERNATIVE METHOD

Knit one piece following the instructions but don't cast off. Knit 1 row on a small stitch size then continue knitting the second side, reversing the shapings. Knit inner mouth in red.

KNITTING SECTIONS TOGETHER

Sections can be joined together on the machine by knitting stitches to stitches or stitches to edges. Occasionally edges are joined by knitting them together on the machine.

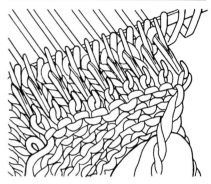

Knitting together: *stitches to stitches.*

TO JOIN STITCHES TO STITCHES

In order to join fabric where the knit sides are facing each other it is necessary to finish both the sections with waste yarn, for example where shoulders are joined, and then re-place both back on the needles with knit sides together. Where the purl sides are to be knitted together, finish one section with waste yarn and leave the second, on completion, on the machine. The first section is then put back on to the needles. With either method the two pieces are knitted together by working one row, then the work is cast off.

Knitting together: *picking up stitches, knit side facing.*

To pick up stitches with the knit side facing

With the knit side facing you, hold the fabric by the waste yarn. Use a single

---

Practice piece shape

Cast off

Increase

Decrease

Mock rib

To make a glove puppet:

1. Sew

2. Fold

3. Sew shaped ends. Then sew sides.

4. Decorate

Glove puppet

Opposite: *Glove puppets are quick to make (p. 45) for gifts or to sell at bazaars.*

pronged transfer tool and push through the 'V's of the last row of stitches knitted in MY. Slide the stitch on to the hook of the needle. Work along the row, placing each stitch on to a needle. Check that the MY stitches are in the hooks. It is easier to see any missed stitches once the waste yarn has been removed. Push the needles back to WP.

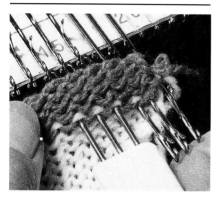

Knitting together: *picking up stitches purl side facing.*

To pick up stitches with the purl side facing

With purl side facing you, hold the fabric by the waste yarn. Using the single pronged transfer tool, push through the fabric under the bar of the last row of stitches in MY. Slide the stitches on to the needles. As the second stitches are placed on the needles, pull the needles out to HP. Unravel the waste yarn and check that all the stitches are on the needles. Thread in MY and knit 1 row using a large stitch size then cast off.

TO JOIN STITCHES AND EDGES
1. With stitches on the machine to join purl sides together.
2. With the edge of the knitting put on to the machine first in order to join

knit sides together. This technique is used to join sleeves finished with waste yarn to the armhole of the garment. It gives a less bulky seam than one formed by sewing together two cast off edges.

Method
When the stitches of one of the pieces are already on the machine, the edge of the fabric is picked up using the 3-pronged transfer tool and placed on to the needles.
Starting at one end of the fabric, insert the tool under the edge chain stitch and place the tool's eyes on to the needle hooks, then pull the needles through the fabric. The edge is then held on the needles.
Repeat the process at the other end of the fabric.
Hang the centre part of the fabric on to the needles either side of 0. The fabric may seem too loose at this point but if the edge is picked up in sections working from the centre of each then the edge will be evenly distributed over the needles. It is not necessary to hook each edge stitch on to a needle.
When the stitches from one piece are not already on the machine, first bring to WP an equivalent number of needles, to the stitches from the second piece. Now hang the fabric edge on to these needles, using the method described above.
The stitches of the second piece are placed on the needles using the appropriate method described in the previous section – joining stitches to stitches. Thread the carriage with MY, knit 1 row in a large stitch size and cast off.

TIP
□ *The sleeves can be joined and knitted to the main garment where the knit side will be used as the 'right' side and when there is no sleeve head shaping. The sleeve is knitted from the shoulder to the cuff.*

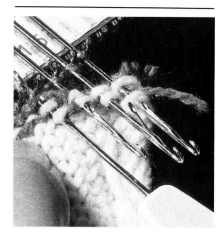

Gathered join: *pick up 1st stitch, then return tool for 2nd stitch.*

GATHERED JOIN

Use
To decrease a number of stitches to give a gathered effect, for example, the cuff of a sleeve or the yoke of a child's dress.
The main section of the sleeve or garment is either started or finished with waste yarn at the gathering line. The cuff or smaller section is knitted and the larger section 'decreased' by putting 2 or 3 stitches together on to each needle as required. The waste yarn is then removed, 1 row knitted then the work is cast off.

TIP
□ *It is very difficult to make a good multiple increase along a row as the stitches become too stretched. It is easier to decrease. If the pattern instructions give such an increase then consider working from the opposite end, for example, shoulder to cuff on a sleeve and so work a multiple decrease at the cuff end of the sleeve, then knit the cuff.*

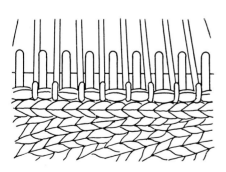

Joining stitches to edges: *pick up only two bars of edge stitch.*

STITCH PATTERN DESIGN

Machine instruction books contain a range of stitch patterns that can be made on the machine either by manual selection or punchcard. In addition to these you can design your own. First draw your design on to squared paper, making each square represent one stitch. Indicate the maximum number of stitches available for one pattern repeat, e.g. 24, and mark the centre squares. Continue the pattern either side of the 24 squares to make sure that the pattern repeats correctly.

Ordinary graph paper does not give a true picture of how the pattern will look when it is knitted as stitches are very rarely square, tending to be wider than they are long. So be prepared to experiment. Some machines can be set to knit each row of the punchcard twice. Once the pattern has been worked out on paper draw it on to the blank punchcard, then make the holes with the special punch. At least 40 rows should be punched in order for a card to rotate properly. It is possible to purchase rolls of punchcard which allow long patterns to be made. The alternative is to join several cards together to make a long loop.

TIP
□ *If you punch a hole in the wrong place pick up a cut-out circle and stick it back in the 'wrong' hole with a small piece of sticky tape.*

WARNING
Do not use the punched out circles as confetti. They are very difficult to remove if accidentally caught in the eyes.

ELECTRONIC MACHINES

When using stitch patterns which are not provided with these machines, the designs are drawn on to special plastic sheets with the special pens or pencils provided by the manufacturer. Only one pattern repeat need be drawn although with small repeating patterns it is best to draw at least 4 rows and 4 stitches. When using a symmetrical pattern, only a quarter of the design need be drawn, then by using the appropriate programme settings, it can be enlarged, mirror imaged and turned upside down to give the complete pattern when knitted. Paper sheets included in the packet of blank plastic sheets enable the pattern to be first drawn and then traced on to the plastic sheet.

FIRST ROW OF PATTERN

Pre-punched cards that come with the punchcard machine have the starting row marked. The knitter sets the card to row I and starts to knit the pattern. The row of punched holes which is visible on the card is not the pattern sequence which will be knitted on the first row. The first row of pattern is already down inside the machine. When punching out your own pattern you may start on the row I that is marked at the side of the new card. If you start the first row of your design on row I this must be fed into the machine before that row will be read. The number of rows that need to be fed into the machine vary from machine to machine.

To find out how many rows need to be in your machine look at a pre-punched card. Find the start of the punched holes of the pattern (one which has a single motif rather than an allover design is the best one to choose). Count the number of rows up to where line I of the pattern is marked. This will be the 6th row up on the Knitmaster, and the 8th row on Brother or Toyota. To start your own card on the first pattern row put the card into the machine and clip the ends together. Move the card round until the first pattern row is immediately above the top of the card feed slot. Turn the card down into the machine either 5 rows for Knitmaster or 7 for Brother and Toyota.

Now when you start to knit, the first row of your design will be the first to knit. Electronic machines are programmed by the knitter to start at the required line.

SETTING UP STITCH PATTERNING

The first step in knitting a stitch pattern is to set the machine to read the pattern. The second step is to set the machine to knit a particular stitch, for example, tuck or Fair Isle. Modern automatic machines require the carriage to cross the needle bed at least once in order to read the pattern, therefore the carriage is set to the stitch pattern before starting the next row. On some machines the needles are selected by operating a lever which allows the stitch selection to be carried out without moving the carriage.

One punchcard can be used to knit several different stitch patterns

although some are only suitable for one type of pattern, for example, lace. Read your instruction book to find out how your machine knits the different pattern stitches. Manufacturers differ in what they name the pattern buttons and levers. The mechanisms involved in the selection and positioning of needles also vary.

Knitmaster machines select and knit the needles as the carriage is moved across, whereas on Brother, Singer and Toyota machines the needles are selected on the previous row leaving them in UWP. On the following row, the pattern is then knitted on those needles, selecting the new pattern needles for the next row.

ROTATING PUNCH CARD PATTERN SELECTION

Step 1: Reading the card
For all makes of machine, feed in card, setting to the first row of pattern, lock on row I. (Electronic machines have no lock setting but automatically read the first row.) Set the levers to read the pattern. Then move the carriage across once.

Step 2: Knitting pattern
Release the card. Set the buttons and levers to the required stitch pattern. Start knitting.
(See top chart p. 66.)

NEEDLE SELECTION WITHOUT KNITTING

This is used to knit in pattern immediately after a welt, or if you need to reset the pattern in order to continue a stitch pattern, for example, the 2nd side of a V neck jumper or after undoing a mistake. The carriage must be moved across the bed to select the pattern needles without knitting a row. The carriage must therefore be set not to knit so that a 'free move' can be made, that is, one where no knitting occurs.
(See middle chart p. 66.)

The selection row must be worked towards the end of the bed where the yarn joins the knitting, therefore two moves of the carriage are usually needed.

COMPARISON OF MANUFACTURERS' NAMES FOR PATTERN SETTING

	BROTHER	KNITMASTER	SINGER	TOYOTA
Step 1: Card reading	KCI KCII SM	Side levers up	Pattern levers	Card Feed Pattern switch
Step 2: Stitch Pattern for:				
Fair Isle	MC	F	colour	F
Tuck	tuck	T	tuck	T
Slip	PART	S	S	EMPTY
Weaving	Step 1 used to set pattern; then weaving brushes put to working position			
Lace on lace carriage	N or F	F	Lace	N

TO RE-SET PATTERN

Move 1: With all needles in WP, re-move yarn from feeder. Disengage pattern selection mechanism (cancel step 1). Set carriage for free move. Move carriage across.

Move 2: Lock card on required row. Leave the carriage set to not knit. Engage the pattern selection mechanism. Move carriage across (step 1). The needles are then selected.

First row of pattern: Release card, Re-thread yarn. Reset RC. Set carriage to knit stitch pattern. Check stitch size. *Note:* If undoing an uneven number of rows the yarn will be at the opposite end to the carriage so there will be no need to work move 1.

PATTERNED GARMENT

The first pattern for a garment knitted in a stitch pattern is a round neck jumper. The front only is worked in tuck stitch with the back and sleeves left plain. New techniques introduced are Holding, Round Neck shaping, Neckbands and Tuck Stitch.

MANUFACTURERS' BUTTON OR LEVER SETTINGS FOR A FREE MOVE

BROTHER	KNITMASTER	SINGER	TOYOTA
Part	Release lever or S	Slip	Empty

HOLDING

Holding is the technique by which some of the stitches in a row remain on the needles without being knitted, while the remaining stitches knit normally. Holding is also known as partial knitting or short rowing.

Uses

1. Shaping, for example, darts, curved hems on skirts, shoulders, necklines.
2. Stitch patterns when the design is worked by keeping needles in hold.
3. Knitting more than 2 colours in a row where only a few stitches of the 3rd colour are required.
4. To make geometric shapes in blocks of colour, this technique is known as Holding Intarsia.

The terms used to indicate the levers which set the carriage on Hold vary between manufacturers. Chart below.

TO PUT NEEDLES INTO HOLDING POSITION (HP)

If more than one needle is to be put into HP *always* have the carriage at op-posite end to the needles – to be moved to position E/D/F. See below.

KNITTING BACK FROM HP

Most modern machines will knit the needles back to WP when the holding levers are set back to normal knitting.

If only a few of the needles in HP are required to knit back then these can be pushed to UWP, but only do so at the opposite end to the carriage. These needles will then knit back to WP as the carriage moves across.

WRAPPING

To avoid holes forming between the stitches in HP and the first stitch of the working stitches, the yarn is wrapped round the first needle in HP either by: *Manual wrapping:* Move the carriage across the knitting and the needles in HP. Take the yarn back by hand under the first needle in HP. Bring the yarn back up between the first and 2nd needle in HP and lay it along top of the

Round neck jumper with tuck stitch front. Knitmaster 360 Card 3 (pattern p. 72 col. 3).

COMPARISON OF MANUFACTURERS' NAMES FOR HOLD SETTING

	BROTHER	KNITMASTER	SINGER	TOYOTA
Name	Lever H	Russel or Front levers	Returning levers	Partial Knitting levers
To Hold	H	I or II	I	I or II
Needle positions	E	D	F	E

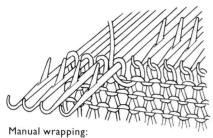

Manual wrapping:
yarn under end needle.

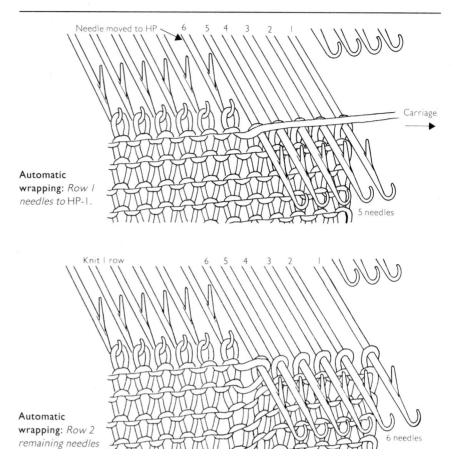

Automatic wrapping: *Row 1 needles to HP-1.*

5 needles

Automatic wrapping: *Row 2 remaining needles to HP.*

6 needles

needles in HP to the carriage. Knit the row. (Do not wrap the yarn round the same needle for more than two rows.) You will see that the yarn is now round the shank of the first needle in HP
or –
Automatic wrapping: Put all but 1 of the needles required into HP. Move the carriage across all the needles. Bring 1 needle forward to HP at the same end as the carriage. Knit the row. You will see that the yarn has been automatically wrapped round the first needle in HP.

TIP
□ *Note that needles in HP without carriage being set to Hold will knit back to WP if a free move is made. Stitches in HP will therefore fall off, avoid this by always setting the carriage to Hold as well as for a free move.*

ROUND NECK SHAPING

The neckline of a garment is shaped by taking the central stitches out of work whilst knitting the shoulder sections. These stitches can either be cast off or held on waste yarn, casting off produces a firm edge while stitches held on waste yarn allow the edge to stretch. Two methods of front neck shaping are given in the instructions below, which also include shoulder shaping.

Practice

This practice piece shows you how to knit a round neck (a small sample) and at the same time to shape the shoulders. The knitting is all in stocking stitch.

Suggested yarn for a standard gauge machine is 4 ply, and for chunky machines, given in brackets [ ], use DK.
Tension: Not too small a stitch, small stitches are difficult to handle. Too large a stitch will give a soft fabric.

Method 1: Cast off neck edge
Back
Cast on with a closed edge over 56 [38] sts.
RC 000. Knit 60 [40] rows.

Shape shoulder:
Row 1: Set carriage to Hold. Put 6 [6] needles to HP at the opposite end to the carriage. Knit across. Manually wrap the first needle in HP.
Repeat this row x 5 [3]. 18 [12] needles in HP at each side of the centre. 20 [14] needles in WP.
Cast off the centre 20 [14] sts.
Push the needles at one side of the centre to UWP.
Knit off with waste yarn. Remove from machine.
Knit the 2nd shoulder stitches on to waste yarn, then remove from the machine.

Front
Cast on with a closed edge over 56 [38] needles.
RC 000. Knit 42 [28] rows.
With carriage at RHS put 31 [21] needles at LHS to HP.
Set carriage to Hold and knit 1 row.
Dec 1 st at neck edge (LHS of working needles) on next and every following alternate row x 7 [5] (last decrease worked when RC reads 55 [37]). Hang claw weights at neck edge while decreasing. Work straight to RC 060 [040].

Shape shoulder:
Shape shoulder as on back, by putting the needles into HP at the armhole edge on alternate rows and at the opposite end to the carriage. The first 6 sts will be put into HP at RC 061 [041] on the RHS of the garment.
When the shoulder shaping is complete push the needles holding shoulder stitches back to UWP.
Knit 1 row with MY. When needles have been wrapped it is easier to pick the stitches up from waste yarn if this extra row is knitted. Knit off with waste yarn. Remove from machine. Put empty needles back to NWP.

Centre neck:
Cast off 6 [4] sts.

2nd side:
Push the remaining 25 [17] needles still in HP back to UWP. Re-thread MY. Set RC to 042 [028].
Knit 1 row.
Decrease 1 st at neck edge on next and every alternate row x 7 [5]. 18 [12] sts remain.
Work to RC 060 [040].
Check the carriage is set to Hold and shape shoulder reversing the shaping of

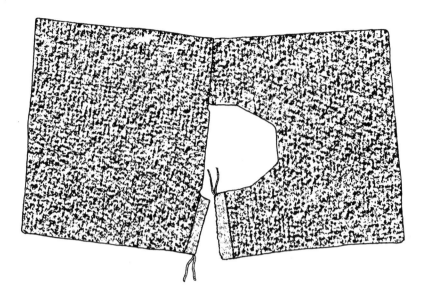

Garment shape for a round neck before neck band added. Note nylon cord.

the first shoulder. Finish with waste yarn. Remove from the machine.
Join one shoulder seam by putting the stitches back on to the machine and knitting off together. (See 'Making up', p. 58.)

This completes a scaled-down practice garment neck. The cast-off edge of the neck is firm which is important where no stretch is required as on a low round neck. You may also notice a mark or 'rub line' where the 2nd side was held while the first was being knitted. This can be avoided by knitting the stitches that would be in the HP position back to NWP with nylon cord.

Knitting on Nylon Cord
Knitting on Nylon Cord is used as an alternative to Holding.

Bring the needles forward so that the stitches are behind the latches. Slowly move the needles back using the straight edge of the needle pusher until the latches are resting against the stitches and lifted slightly.
Lay the nylon cord in the needle hooks. Push the needles back so that the latches close.
Hold the short end of the nylon cord and knit back one stitch at a time. Pull a long loop through and push the needle back to NWP.
Make sure that the stitch already knitted is not pulled forward. The nylon stitches will now take the rub.
To reduce the rub even further either

put a strip of sticky tape along the sinker posts or hang a thin strip of knitting on to the sinker posts. The latter has the advantage that the fabric is held back against the sinker posts and the nylon stitches remain in NWP.
To return the stitches to WP remove any protecting strip, hold both ends of the nylon cord and pull the long end firmly so that the needles move forward to the edge of the bed just between the sinker posts.
Pull the nylon cord sharply and firmly upwards and slightly to the back of the machine (as if undoing unwanted rows) and take it from the needle hooks. The stitches are then lined up in WP ready to start knitting.

Centre neck stitches on a nylon cord. Pick up side neck stitches.

Method 2: Holding stitches on waste yarn
Back:
Work as given for method 1 until shoulder shaping is complete. 18 [12] sts in HP on each shoulder with 20 [14] sts in WP at the centre back. The shoulders and centre stitches must now be knitted in waste yarn. Push the shoulder needles at the opposite end to the carriage to UWP. Knit 1 row. Break yarn. Bring the 20 [14] needles in the centre to HP. Knit 6–8 rows with waste yarn on first shoulder then remove from machine.
Push the centre needles to UWP and knit 6–8 rows in waste yarn then remove from machine.
Re-thread MY. Cancel HP setting. Knit 1 row across shoulder stitches. Break yarn.
Thread waste yarn and knit 6–8 rows as before.

Front:
Work as given for method 1 up to the neck shaping.
Bring the 31 [21] needles to HP (or UWP) but knit the stitches on to the nylon cord. Instead of decreasing knit each stitch back with the end of the nylon cord. (*Hint:* If you do not have a long enough cord then use a length of strong yarn.)
Work the shoulder shaping as before.

2nd side:
Carefully pull back the nylon cord holding the 25 [17] stitches of the shoulder and the neck to WP. 13 [9] stitches will remain in the centre, held on the nylon cord.
Shape the 2nd side as given for the first, knitting the decrease stitches back with nylon cord. Finish with waste yarn.

Centre and neck edge:
Put the centre stitches back into the needle hooks and remove nylon cord. Hold the remaining edge of the neck out at either side of the centre stitches. Using the 3-pronged/single pronged transfer tool, pick up about 8 [4] stitches along each edge. Knit 1 row with MY. Knit off with waste yarn. Join one shoulder seam.
Now, using the two practice garments, try out the neckbands that are set out below.

NECKBANDS

Neckbands are either knitted directly on to the garment or knitted separately then joined on afterwards. Many people find difficulty in gauging the number of stitches required to knit a neat

neckband. Here are several methods to try:

1. Hold the neck of the garment up to the needle bed without stretching it and estimate the number of needles to use.
2. Measure the neck edge and calculate the number of stitches required based on the MT of the garment. The neckband is knitted on a smaller stitch size which means that the number calculated using the MT figure makes the finished band sufficiently tight.
3. Use the stitches on waste yarn where the neckline was shaped by using the holding method (Method 2).

KNITTING NECKBANDS

Method: Picking up the edge

With the side of the work that will be worn as the outside of the garment towards you, hold the cast-off edge of the neck up to the needle bed. Using the 3-pronged transfer tool hook one end of the neck on to the needles.
Estimate, or calculate, the number of needles needed, then hook the other end of the neck on to the needles. Distribute the width of neck edge evenly across the needles. Make sure that the same number of needles is used on either side of the centre front.
Thread MY into the carriage and knit 1 row MT.

If you have difficulty in knitting this row:
1. Check that the garment is not caught in the carriage wheels.
2. Try pushing all needles to HP before you start.
3. Knit each stitch across by hand, starting at the opposite end to the carriage.

Neckbands can be knitted in stocking stitch over all the needles or as a 1 x 1 or 2 x 2 mock rib, or in fact any other needle setting you wish, but the first row must be worked over all the needles after which the appropriate stitches are transferred.

KNITTING NECKBAND WITH CAST-OFF NECK EDGE

Method: Knitting band 1

Pick up the stitches needed – about 56 [36]. Using MY work 1 row MT.
Knit 8 [5] rows MT − 2, 1 row MT + 2, 8 [5] rows MT − 2.
Knit 1 row MT. Finish with waste yarn.

Small-scale samples illustrating round neckbands. (From top) Band 1, Band 2, Band 3, Band 5.

Remove from machine. Join 2nd shoulder.
Press last row of MY and waste yarn. Fold band in half to the front of the garment, then working through each stitch, backstitch into place, unravelling the waste yarn as you sew.

TIP
□ *To make a neat seam on a neckband, work over one extra needle at each end of the band. The extra stitches are then used in the seam when sewing up the band. Make sure that these needles do not carry any neck edge stitches.*

Method: Knitting band 2

The stitches for this band are picked up as for band 1 except that the side of the garment that will be worn outside (the right side) is away from the knitter. The band is knitted and finished in the same way but the sewing down is different. The band will fold to the inside of the garment. The stitches are then sewn in place with slipstitch.

Method: Knitting band 3

This is worked as band 2 but cast off loosely instead of finishing with waste yarn. The cast off edge is slipstitched into place. This gives a firm edge which may not stretch enough.

KNITTING NECKBAND WITH NECK HELD ON WASTE YARN

Method: Knitting band 4

Knit either as given for band 1 or band 2. Both bands will have an elastic finish.

Method: Knitting band 5

Cast on and knit the band first, then attach the garment to it by knitting or sewing. The amount of stitches needed are calculated, or estimated, as for band 1, but the garment is removed from the needles.
Bring the required number of needles to WP and arrange needle selection for stocking stitch or mock rib.
Cast on with waste yarn and knit 6–8 rows.
Knit 1 row with nylon cord.
Knit mock rib or hem at MT − 2 for the required depth, say 8 [5] rows when using the practice garments. Make a turning row at MT + 2, then the 2nd side of the mock rib or hem at MT − 2.
Join the rib or hem and knit 1 row across all needles. Do not take off machine if joining to the garment by knitting.
If you wish to sew the neckband in place then finish on waste yarn, and then backstitch evenly to the outside of the garment.

KNITTING NECKBAND TO GARMENT

either
1. Hang the neck edge on to the needles with the right side of garment facing you, use MY, knit 1 row MT then 2–4 rows MT − 2. Break MY leaving a long edge. Thread with waste yarn and knit 6–8 rows. Take off machine. Backstitch last row of MY to front of garment.
or
2. With inside of garment facing, knit 1 row with a large stitch size and latch off loosely.

TUCK

Features of this type of stitch are:
1. A textured pattern usually worn with the purl side outside.
2. Knitted in smooth or silky yarns, the patterns produced show much more clearly.
3. An open lace-like fabric is formed by using the tuck stitch patterning with some needles out of work. This is known as tuck lace.
4. Coloured stripes knitted in tuck stitch give the appearance of 2 colours in one row.
5. Can be used with a ribber to knit Fisherman's rib and other textured patterns.

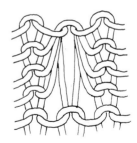

Tuck stitch

Tuck stitch produces a shorter and wider piece of fabric than that produced by stocking stitch when the same yarn, stitch size, number of stitches and rows are used. The number of loops of yarn able to be held in the needle and collected on each row, to form the tucked stitches, will vary with the stitch size and yarn thickness. If too many are held they will not knit off to finish the tuck. Most tuck stitch patterns have one stitch tucking between non-tucking, plain stitches. (In tuck lace there may be a gap between the needle tucking and the plain knitting needle where a needle is an NWP.) Some machines will tuck over 2 adjacent needles. Always try a sample if knitting a familiar tuck pattern with a new yarn.

KNITTING TUCK

Tuck can be worked on all machines *either*

Manually: The needles which make the tuck stitch are put into HP and the carriage set to hold.
or

Punchcard: Using a pre-punched pattern card the needles, which will make the tuck stitches, are automatically selected. The pattern selection row is worked, then the carriage is set to tuck and the knitting started.

PRACTICE: TUCK STITCH

Manual selection

Cast on over about 40 [20] needles. Work 4 rows stocking stitch.

Row 1: Push every alternate needle into HP. Set the machine to Hold. Knit 1 row.

Row 2: Cancel the Hold setting or push the needles to UWP. Knit 1 row. Repeat rows 1 and 2 x 10. Make sure that you always push the same needles to HP each time. Knit 6 rows plain.

Punchcard selection

Select the card that has the following stitch pattern arrangement:

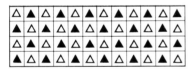

Feed in card and lock on 1 row.

Row 1: Knit to select pattern.

Row 2: Set carriage to tuck. Do not release card.
Knit across.

Row 3: Cancel tuck button. Knit 1 row. Repeat rows 2 and 3 x 10. Knit 6 rows plain.
Compare this section with the first section.
Note which needles are tucking and the different way in which the needles

move to make tuck stitch.
To find out on your machine, whether either the holes or the blanks in the punchcard represent the tuck stitches, take a card from the basic set, the instructions or pattern book will show which cards are suitable for tuck. Choose a punchcard which has more holes than blanks, then knit a length of the pattern and note which stitches tuck – compare this with the punchcard.

TIP
□ *The centre of the punchcard corresponds with the centre of the needle bed.*

Try your own punchcards

1. Make a sampler of all the cards recommended for tuck in the pattern book with your machine. Keep a record of the yarn and stitch size used.
2. Take a card and set the machine to only tuck when the carriage is moved in one direction. For Brother and Singer machines: push down only 1 tuck button, for Toyota: set tuck to single arrow either left or right, and for Knitmaster: put 1 side lever up, the other down or set the carriage to T for one row then back to O for the next.
3. Lock the card on row 1. Try tucking for 3 rows then work 1 row with no tuck setting.
4. Double the length of the pattern, and therefore the tucked stitches, where there is a 'doubling' switch.

ROUND NECK JUMPER

This garment is constructed in the same way as the slash neck jumper with the addition of round neck shaping. The front of the garment is knitted in tuck stitch.

STANDARD GAUGE MACHINE

Sizes: 40(42,44) in/102(107,112) cm chest/bust.

Yarn: 400 g 4 ply acrylic.

Tension: 27.5 sts and 38.5 rows to 10 cm square over stocking stitch. 22.5 sts and 62 rows to 10 cm square over tuck stitch.

Stitch pattern:

O	O	O	▲	O	O	O	▲	O	O	O	▲
O	O	O	▲	O	O	O	▲	O	O	O	▲
O	O	O	▲	O	O	O	▲	O	O	O	▲
O	O	O	▲	O	O	O	▲	O	O	O	▲
O	▲	O	O	O	▲	O	O	O	▲	O	O
O	▲	O	O	O	▲	O	O	O	▲	O	O
O	▲	O	O	O	▲	O	O	O	▲	O	O
O	▲	O	O	O	▲	O	O	O	▲	O	O

▲ needles forming tuck stitch
O needles knitting normally

Any tuck pattern card can be used but it is important to obtain the correct tension.

Back

Work in stocking stitch.
Cast on 160(174,182) sts with waste yarn for 2 x 1 mock rib. Knit 6–8 rows.
Work 1 row with nylon cord.
Change to MY.
Work 20 rows MT − 2, 1 row MT + 2, 20 rows MT − 2.
Pick up hem. Work 1 row at MT + 2.
Set RC to 000. Knit straight to RC 116(120,124).
Mark the end stitches with a length of contrast yarn.
Continue knitting straight to RC 220(228,236).
At the same end as the carriage leave 55(62,65) needles in WP.
Push the remaining needles to HP. Set the carriage to Hold for partial knitting.
Knit the stitches in WP with waste yarn for 6–8 rows.
Remove these stitches from the machine.
At the opposite end of the work, push 55(62,65) of the needles back to UWP. Knit these back to WP with waste yarn, then work 6–8 rows more. Remove these stitches from the machine. Cancel the partial knitting setting on the carriage. With waste yarn knit the remaining 50(50,52) stitches. Knit 6–8 rows. Remove from the machine.

Front

Work in tuck stitch.
Cast on 132(140,146) stitches. Knit 2 x 1 mock rib as given for back.
Note: As tuck stitch knitting makes a wider fabric than the same number of stitches in stocking stitch, fewer stitches are needed to give the same width. Because of this the front welt of the jumper has fewer stitches than the back welt so that the width of the fabric in tuck stitch pattern will be the same as the width of the stocking stitch back. The difference in width of the welts is not noticeable when the finished garment is being worn.

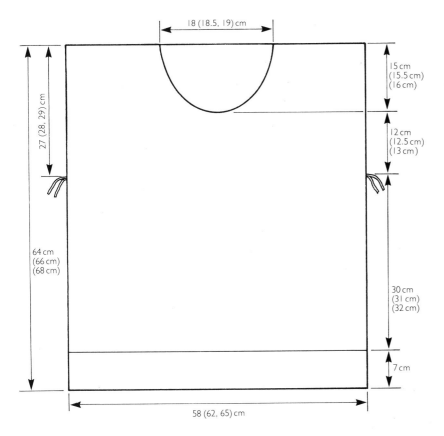

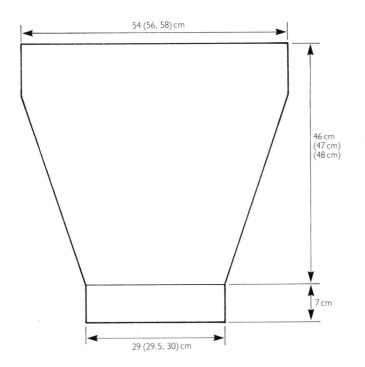

Round Neck Jumper:
Sizes 40 (42, 44) in chest/Sizes 102 (107, 112) cm chest

TIP
□ *If using an automatic punch card machine, use the hem joining row to set the pattern after working the welt rows; i.e., feed in card, lock on first row, set carriage to read the card, then knit the joining row at MT+2.*

Set RC to 000. Set carriage to tuck. Use MT for tuck stitch. Knit in pattern to RC 186(192,198).
Mark the end stitches with a length of contrast yarn. Continue in pattern to RC 260(270,278).

Shape neck

Set RC to 000. Work the first side of the neck. Either side can be worked first but instructions are given here for working the RHS first.

TIP
□ *Always work the same side as the carriage first which will save breaking and re-joining yarn.*

At LHS, and using nylon cord, knit back by hand 73(77,87) sts to NWP. To prevent the carriage brushes rubbing the fabric as it passes to and fro, either hang a strip of waste knitting from the sinker posts or place a length of sticky tape across the base of the stitches on the nylon cord.
Carriage at RHS. NOTE AND RECORD THE ROW NUMBER of the pattern showing at the punch card feed slot.
Continue knitting in pattern as follows:
Reset RC 000. Knit 1 row. Hang claw weights at edges of knitting, moving them up as needed.
RC 001. Dec 1 st at neck edge on this and every following 4th row x 5 (6 sts in all decreased).
RC 021. Dec 1 st at neck edge on every following 6th row x 5 (11 sts decreased).
RC 051. Dec 1 st at neck edge on every following 8th row x 2 (13 sts decreased).
RC 067. Work straight to RC 094(096,100). Break yarn.
Knit the remaining 46(50,53) sts with waste yarn for 6–8 rows. Remove from machine. Push the empty needles back to NWP.
At the LHS of the work remove the stitch protection strip and bring the first 59(63,66) needles back to WP.
The centre 14(14,16) stitches remain in NWP on nylon cord. Replace stitch protection strip.

Selecting the correct row of the pattern

Set the punchcard to the pattern row number recorded before starting *cont.*

Above: *A selection of tuck stitch samples. (From top) Knitmaster 360, card 12A, colour changed every 2 rows; then same card, single colour; Knitmaster card 3, 2 colours changed every 4 rows; Knitmaster card 3, 3 colours changed every 4 rows (stitch pattern p. 72, col. 3); for Knitmaster card 1, 3 colours changed every 2 rows, see pp. 10–11, top 3 samples.*
Right: *Child's round neck jumper knitted with tuck stitch front on a Chunky machine. Knitmaster card 3 (stitch pattern p. 72, col. 3).*

to shape the first side. Lock the card at this number with the carriage at the RHS, set the carriage to read the card but not to knit i.e. press the slip, empty, part or carriage release button as appropriate. All the needles must be in WP. With no yarn in feeder take the carriage across.

Release the card and set RC to 000. Thread yarn into carriage, set the carriage to tuck and knit the second side to match the first.

The carriage will start to knit from the LHS but the pattern will read the same although set from a different side.

Centre neck

Remove stitch protection strip. Bring remaining 14(14,16) sts forward to WP. Remove nylon cord, then finish off with 6–8 rows in waste yarn. Remove from the machine.

Joining one shoulder seam

Join pieces together with the purl side of front facing the knit side of back. Hook the 55(62,65) sts from one back shoulder on to the needles, placing a stitch on every needle. There are more stitches on the back shoulder than there are on the front shoulder. Distribute 46(50,53) stitches from the front shoulder evenly over the needles carrying the back stitches, leaving some needles with only one stitch. To avoid holes in the seam, pick up the heel of an adjacent stitch and hook it on to a needle carrying only one stitch. Knit 1 row using a large stitch size and cast off.

Neckband

With inside of garment facing, pick up the 50(50,52) sts from the back. Use the 3 pronged transfer tool and pick up between 40 and 45 stitches from 1 side of front neck, 14 sts from centre front and an equal number from 2nd side of neck. Remove waste yarn and using MY, knit 1 row.

Then arrange the stitches for a 2 × 1 mock rib by transferring every 3rd stitch to its adjacent needle. To shape the neckband so that it lies flat at the neck edge, alter the stitch size on every other row.

To work a neckband 16 rows deep:

Work 2 rows MT − 2 (hem/welt stitch size).
Work 2 rows MT − 2 • (1 dot tighter tension).
Work 2 rows MT − 2 •• (2 dots tighter tension, i.e., smaller stitch).
Work 2 rows MT − 3 and so on to MY − 4.

Knit 1 row at MT + 2 to give a turning row then work another 14 rows gradually increasing the stitch size on every

alternate row to return to MT − 2. The neckband is finished with waste yarn.

Join the second shoulder seam, distributing the front stitches as before. Sew down the neckband by slipstitching each stitch held on waste yarn evenly to the inside of the garment.

Sleeves

First sleeve: With the inside of the garment facing (the knit side of the front and the purl side of the back) and using the 3 pronged transfer tool, hook the armhole edge on to 150(156,162) needles, i.e. 75(78,81) each side of the centre shoulder seam down to the marker threads.

Set RC to 000. Thread the machine. Knitting in stocking stitch, work 1 row at MT + 2 then return to MT and work 20 rows straight.

RC 021. Dec 1 st each end on next and every following 4th row × 15(21,22). RC 76(104,108). 120(114,118) stitches remaining.

Work 4 rows straight, then dec 1 st each end of next and every following 5th row × 20(16,16).
RC 180(184,188). 80(82,84) stitches remaining.

Arrange needles for 2 × 1 mock rib and knit cuff as back welt. Finish on waste yarn.
Repeat for second sleeve.

Making up

Join side and sleeve seams. Turn cuffs under and slipstitch into place. Do not press.

CHUNKY MACHINE

Sizes: 28(30,32) in/71(76,81) cm chest.

Yarn: 400 g double knit.

Tension over stocking stitch: 19 sts and 29 rows to 10 cm square.

Tension over tuck stitch: 15 sts and 45 rows to 10 cm square.

Stitch pattern:

Any tuck card or pattern may be worked but it is important to obtain the correct tension.

Back

Work in stocking stitch.
Cast on 73(77,83) sts with waste yarn for 1 × 1 mock rib. Knit 6–8 rows.
Work 1 row with nylon cord.
Change to MY.
Work 12 rows MT − 2, 1 row MT + 2, 12 rows MT − 2.
Pick up hem. Work 1 row at MT + 2.
Set RC to 000 MT. Knit straight to RC 052(060, 064).
Mark the end stitches with a length of contrast yarn. Continue knitting straight to RC 104(112,120).
At the same end as the carriage leave 24 (26,29) needles in WP.
Push the remaining needles to HP. Set the carriage to Hold for partial knitting.
Knit the stitches in WP with waste yarn for 6–8 rows.
Remove these stitches from the machine.
At the opposite end of the work, push 24(26,29) of the needles back to UWP. Knit these back to WP with waste yarn, then work 6–8 rows more. Remove these stitches from the machine. Cancel the Hold setting on the carriage. Knit 6–8 rows with waste yarn over the remaining 25 stitches. Remove from the machine.

Front

Work in tuck stitch.
Cast on 57(61,65) stitches. Knit 1 × 1 mock rib as given for back.

Note: As tuck stitch knitting makes a wider fabric than the same number of stitches in stocking stitch, fewer stitches are needed to give the same width. Because of this the front welt of the jumper has fewer stitches than the back welt so that the width of the fabric in tuck stitch pattern will be the same as the width of the stocking stitch back. The difference in width of the welts is not noticeable when the finished garment is being worn.

TIP
□ *If using an automatic punchcard machine, use the hem joining row to set the pattern after working the welt rows; i.e., feed in card, lock on first row, set carriage to read the card, then knit the joining row at MT + 2.*

Set RC to 000. Set carriage to tuck. Use MT for tuck stitch. Knit in pattern to RC 80(96,100).
Mark the end stitches with a length of contrast yarn.
Continue in pattern to RC 130(146,154).

cont.

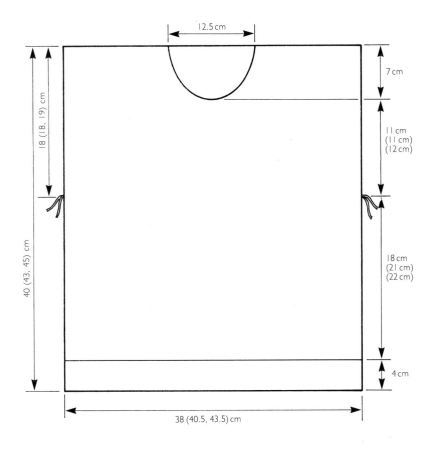

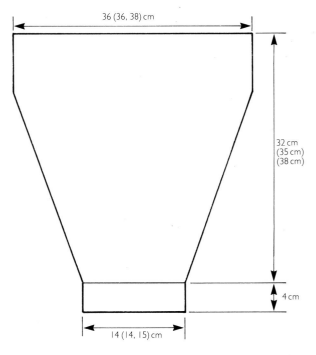

Round Neck Jumper:
Sizes 28 (30, 32) in chest/Sizes 71 (76, 81) cm chest

Shape neck

Set RC to 000. Work the first side of the neck. Either side can be worked first but instructions are given here for working the RHS first.

TIP
□ *Always work the same side as the carriage first to save breaking and rejoining yarn.*

At LHS, and using nylon cord, knit back by hand 32(34,40) sts to NWP. To prevent the carriage brushes rubbing the fabric as it passes to and fro, either hang a strip of waste knitting from the sinker posts or place a length of sticky tape across the base of the stitches not being worked.
Carriage at RHS. NOTE AND RECORD THE ROW NUMBER of the pattern showing at the punch card feed slot.

Continue knitting in pattern as follows:
Reset RC 000. Knit 1 row. Hang claw weights at edges of knitting, moving them up as needed.
RC 001. Dec 1 st at neck edge on this and every following 3rd row x 4 (4 sts in all decreased).
RC 010. Knit 6 rows.
RC 016. Dec 1 st at neck edge on this and following 8th row.
RC 026. Work straight to RC 032. Break yarn. Knit the remaining sts with waste yarn for 6–8 rows. Remove from machine. Push the empty needles back to NWP.
At the LHS of the work remove the stitch protection strip and bring the first 30(32,35) needles back to WP. The centre 7 stitches remain in NWP on nylon cord.
Replace stitch protection strip.

To select the correct row of the pattern:
Set the punchcard to show the pattern row number recorded before starting to shape the first side. Lock the card at this number with the carriage at RHS, set the carriage to read the card but not to knit, i.e., press the slip, empty, part or carriage release button as appropriate. All the needles must be in WP. With no yarn in feeder take the carriage across.
Release the card and set RC to 000. Thread yarn into carriage, set the carriage to tuck and knit the second side to match the first.
The carriage will start to knit from the LHS but the pattern will read the same, although set from a different side.

Centre neck

Remove stitch protection strip. Bring remaining 7 sts to WP. Remove   *cont.*

nylon cord, then finish off with 6–8 rows in waste yarn. Remove from the machine.

Joining one shoulder seam

Join pieces together with the purl side of front facing the knit side of back. Hook the 24(26,29) sts from one back shoulder on to the needles, placing a stitch on every needle. There are more stitches on the back shoulder than there are on the front shoulder. Distribute 19(21,23) stitches from the front shoulder evenly over the needles carrying the back stitches, leaving some needles with only one stitch. To avoid holes in the seam, pick up the heel of an adjacent stitch and hook it on to a needle carrying only one stitch. Knit 1 row using a large stitch and cast off.

Neckband

With inside of garment facing, pick up 25 sts from the back. Use the 3 pronged transfer tool and pick up about 16 stitches from 1 side of front neck, 7 sts from centre front and an equal number from 2nd side of neck. Remove waste yarn and using MY, knit 1 row. Either leave the stitches for a plain stocking stitch neckband or arrange the stitches for a 1 × 1 mock rib by transferring every 2nd stitch to its adjacent needle.
Work the neckband 8 rows deep at MT − 2, then finish with waste yarn and remove from the machine.

Finishing the 2nd shoulder

When the neckband has been completed, measure the length of the neckband slightly stretched. It should be able to stretch to at least 50 cm to allow a child's head to go through. If it is not wide enough, then an opening on the shoulder should be made which can be closed in wear with press studs or a button.
To work an open shoulder, pick up the stitches from the back of the garment with the purl side facing and hang them on to the needles. Knit 8 rows in stocking stitch and cast off. Return the stitches on the front shoulder to the needles, work 1 row then cast off. Join the shoulder edge of the flap to the front of the garment. If not all of the shoulder opening is required, then part of it can be sewn down.
If a shoulder opening is not required, then join the 2nd shoulder in the same way as the first.

Sleeves

First sleeve: With the inside of the garment facing (the knit side of the front and the purl side of the back) and using the 3 pronged transfer tool, hook the

armhole edge on to 68(68,72) needles, i.e. 34(34,36) each side of the centre shoulder seam down to the marker threads.
Set RC to 000. Thread the machine. Knitting in stocking stitch, work 1 row at MT + 2 then return to MT and work 11(21,11) rows straight.
RC 012(022,012). Dec 1 st each end on next and every following 4th(4th,5th) row until 30(30,32) sts remain. RC 84(94,104).
Work 1 row. Arrange needles for 1 × 1 mock rib and knit cuff as back welt. Finish on waste yarn.
Repeat for second sleeve.

Making up

Join side and sleeve seams. Turn neckband and cuffs under and slipstitch into place. Sew on button and make loop to finish shoulder opening if required.

DESIGNING YOUR OWN PATTERNS

A garment pattern can be made in two ways:
1. By drawing the shape and using a charting device.
2. By calculation.

THE CHARTING DEVICE

Knitmaster's Knit-Radar, Singer's Knit Copy, Brother's Knitleader, Toyota's Knit Tracer.
These devices can either be built into the machine or added as an extra. A charting device is well worth having if you wish to experiment with your own designs or knit a given pattern in a different yarn.
Many magazines give block diagrams – the drawn shapes of the garment sections – with measurements. These diagrams can be drawn on special paper used with the charter.
The charting device consists of a roller with a mechanism to rotate the chart, the chart itself, either a printed pattern or a blank sheet on which you can draw your own pattern, and a set of stitch scales. The pattern is drawn to half or full scale. A tension swatch of 40 [20] stitches and 60 [30] rows must be

It is easy to design your own garments. Start by adapting a known pattern.

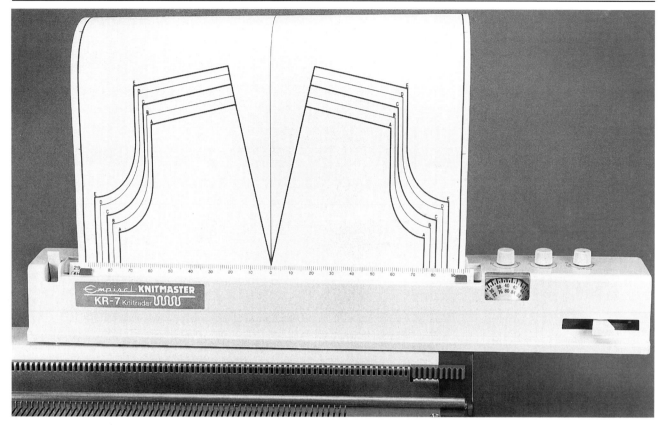

Knitmaster charting device added to a standard gauge machine. Other makes and models have the device built-in. It is used when you knit your own designs or knit different stitch patterns and yarns.

knitted and measured before using the drawn shape.

A stitch scale is selected and slotted in the front of the charter, under the line drawing of the pattern piece. The measurement of rows is set to determine the rate at which the roller will move the chart as the carriage passes to and fro across the knitting, triggering the device each time.

As the knitting proceeds the lines indicating the edges of the pattern piece on the chart pass behind the stitch scale and show row by row the shaping required.

TIP

□ *If you are uncertain of the evenness of the shaping, then try running the chart through the machine first by moving the carriage without any yarn. This is a dry or practice run.*

CALCULATION

Where there is no charting device the shaping must be calculated mathematically. It is more complicated, but most knitted fabric is very accommodating and, provided the shape achieved at the finish is acceptable to the wearer, it is well worth having a try. Not too much time need be spent calculating.

DRAWING A ROUND NECK SHAPE

Construct a rectangle of the width of the back neck by the depth required at the centre front neck of the garment.

BACK NECK MEASUREMENT

Chest/bust size in inches	Measurement of garment back neck in cm
18	9
20	9.5
22	9.5
24	10
26	11
28	11
30	12.5
32	14
34	14.5
36	15
38	15.5
40	16
42	16
44	16.5
46	17.5

STANDARD NECK DEPTH FOR ROUND NECK OF GARMENT

Infant	2.5 cm
Child	5 cm
Woman	7.5 cm
Man	10 cm

Draw the curve as indicated on to the diagram (opposite, top).
This is for a round neck with the band at the base of the neck. You need to take into account what the finished neck line will be and subtract the depth of the ribbed band if a lower neck is required. For polo neck jumpers, make the neckline about 1 cm deeper than the natural neckline.

Remember to find out what the finished neck opening will measure when knitting round neck jumpers for children. A shoulder opening may look better than a neckband big enough to go over the head.

DRAWING A CURVE

To calculate the curve for neck shaping using the tension information.
1. Find out the number of rows required for the neck depth.

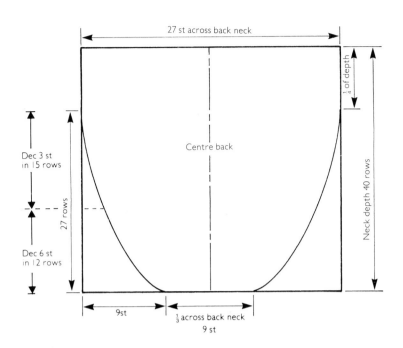

How to draw a curve for a round neck.

2. Calculate the number of rows in the shaped section. Take three quarters of the rows needed for the neck depth.
3. Work out the number of stitches required for the back neck measurement.
4. Calculate the number of stitches to be decreased in shaping the neck, then take one third of the number of stitches required for back neck width.

Example

The number of rows to give neck depth = 40.
Therefore the number of rows required for shaping is $\frac{3}{4} \times 40 = 30$.
The number of stitches to given back neck width = 27.
Therefore the number of stitches required for shaping is $\frac{1}{3} \times 27 = 9$.
So to obtain the curve, 9 stitches will be decreased over 30 rows.

An appropriate guide to how the shaping is to be done is to halve the number of rows, then divide the stitches so that two thirds of the stitches are decreased over the first half of the rows and the other one third of stitches over the remaining rows. In the above example 6 stitches (two third's of 9) could be decreased over about the first 15 rows and the 3 (one third of 9) over the second 15 rows. These stitches decreased 1 st every alternate row over the next 12 rows, followed by 1st every 5th row over the following 15 rows would given an acceptable curve.

SLIP OR SKIP STITCHES

A pattern is formed where stitches are not knitted and 'floats' of yarn are carried under the missed stitch or stitches across the surface of the fabric. The setting for slip stitch enables the carriage to be moved across the bed from one side to the other without the stitches

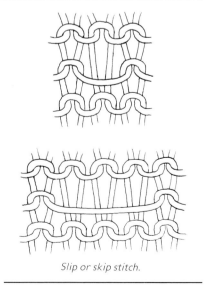

Slip or skip stitch.

either knitting or falling off, i.e. a free move. This is used where rows have been unravelled so leaving the carriage at the opposite end of the work to the yarn, or to where the stitch pattern is to be set without actually knitting the row. Some Knitmaster machines have a Carriage Release lever which is used for this purpose, other machines use the Slip, Empty or Part button. (See p. 66.)

TIP
□ *All the needles must be in WP or HP with the carriage set to Hold when the carriage is moved across. Needles left in the UWP will drop their stitches if no yarn is in the carriage. Removing the yarn from the carriage on a free move prevents it getting caught under the carriage.*

USING ONE COLOUR

Slip stitch patterning using one colour only produces textured fabric. The pattern shows on the purl side of the fabric, where between two and six stitches are slipped next to each other at regular intervals along the row, then this row is repeated at least once more. It is not advisable to have more than six stitches slipped together as the long floats formed can catch and pull in wear. Light coloured and silky textured yarns show the patterns to their best advantage. Compared with a stocking stitch fabric using the same yarn, number of stitches and rows, the slip stitch patterning will produce a much shorter and thicker fabric, which can also be narrower.

USING TWO COLOURS

Slip stitches using two colours can best be achieved with punchcards which have a pattern where every two rows are identical; or, this can also be achieved using any card where machines can be set to repeat the same row twice. On the Brother and Toyota use the card lock lever put on to the V (elongated triangle) mark, and on the Knitmaster set the card lock lever to 'L'.

The colours are alternated every two rows and the pattern which results can be very different from that formed when knitting two colours together along one row as in Fair Isle. Try working with a pattern card, as indicated in your pattern book, suitable for 2 colour slip stitch patterns. It is not always necessary to set the card lock to the double row setting.

USING THREE COLOURS

Three colours can be knitted in one row by using slip stitches. The pattern is punched on to the card, each colour

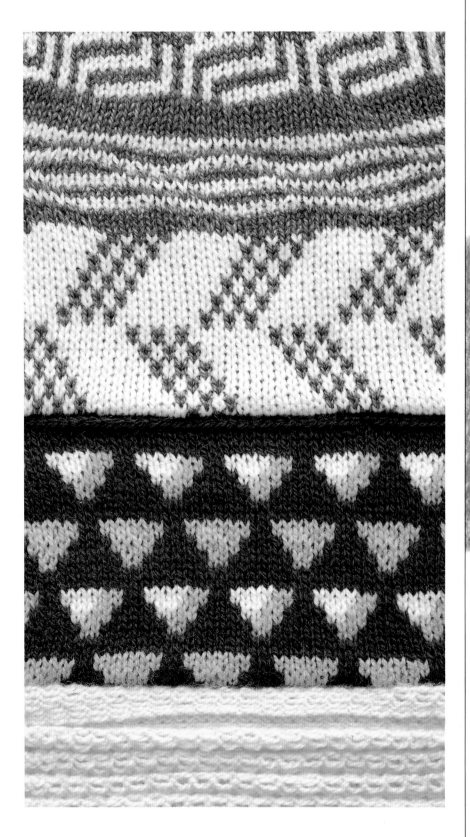

Above: *Slip stitch samples. (From top) 2 colour slip pattern; an alternative 2 colour slip pattern; for comparison, same card using Fair Isle setting (Brother 840 card 9A); 3 colour slip pattern using Brother pattern 363 (p. 119 of book 4); tea cosy slipstitch using card 1 on most machines (stitch pattern p. 72, col. 1); for 1 colour slip pattern silky yarn, see pp. 10–11, bottom sample (stitch pattern p. 84).*

Right: *Classic style round neck jumper (pp. 62–78) with set-in sleeves (pp. 84–5) knitted in slipstitch. Brother 840 card 9A; Knitmaster 360 card 5 (stitch pattern p. 84).*

worked individually and over two rows at a time. This means that in order to complete two rows of knitting with three colours six movements of the carriage across the bed are needed (two with each colour).

MAKING A RUCHED OR RIDGED FABRIC

This fabric is made by knitting 1 row of a pattern repeatedly where several stitches are slipped; the slip stitches produce a thick decorative fabric. If worked in stripes of colour this pattern gives an interesting honeycomb fabric with little pockets of colour.

Many combinations of this technique can be made; the simplest is known either as teacosy or ridge stitch. It is made by using a card with alternate needles slipping; this can be done by manual selection, the same needles being selected for 4–10 rows, depending on the height of ridge required. Two rows of plain stocking stitch are knitted between the ridges. When a punchcard is used it is locked on one row. The machine is set to slip for 4–10 rows then to knit stocking stitch for 2 rows.

SLIP STITCH SETTINGS WITH THE RIBBING ATTACHMENT

Double bed jacquard produces a two colour pattern similar to Fair Isle, but there are no floats as these are knitted in by the other bed making a double thickness fabric.

Pin Tucks and Raised Ridge Patterns are made by knitting on one bed and slipping the pattern needles on the other.

Practice

Try the slip stitch patterns shown in your instruction book. The slip stitch setting is very useful and a much neglected feature of modern knitting machines.

SLIP STITCH AND SET-IN SLEEVES

This pattern is for a round neck jumper with set-in sleeves, worked in slip stitch pattern throughout.

Sizes: 34(36,38) in//86(91,97) cm chest/bust.

Yarn: 300 g 3 ply acrylic.

Tension: 31.5 sts and 64 rows to 10 cm.

Stitch pattern:

● slip stitch   ○ plain stocking stitch

Punch each row twice or use double row switch.
See Brother card no 5, Knitmaster card no 9.

Back

Cast on for 2 × 1 mock rib over 155(161,170) needles.
Work mock rib 26 rows deep at MT − 2 (26 rows + 1 turning row + 26 rows).
Join mock rib.
Inc 1 (1,0) st. 156 (162,170) sts.
Work 1 row at MT + 2 and set machine for pattern.
RC 000. Set carriage to slip. MT. Knit to RC 194(198, 200).

Shape armholes:

Cast off 8(8,9) sts at beginning of next 2 rows.
Cast off 4 sts at beginning of the next 2 rows.
Dec 1 st at each end of the next 2 rows.
Dec 1 st at each end of next and following alternate row. Knit 4 rows.
Dec 1 st at each end of next row. Knit 6 rows.
Dec 1 st at each end of next row. 120(126,132) sts.
Knit to RC 324(338,352).

Shape shoulders:

Set machine to Hold.
Put 5 needles to HP at opposite end to carriage on each of the next 12 rows.
Put 6(8,10) needles to HP at the opposite end to the carriage on the next 2 rows.
Finish each set of the 36(38,40) shoulder sts and the centre 48(50,52) sts separately by knitting on to waste yarn.
Remove work from the machine.

Front

Work as given for back to RC 282(294,306).

Shape neck:

For the first side work on the end 50(53,56) sts.

Put 70(73,76) needles to HP or NWP (knit them on to nylon cord).
Record the pattern row number and RC reading.
Work 1 row.
Dec 1 st at neck edge on next and every alternate row × 11.
Dec 1 st at neck edge on every following 4th row × 3(4,5).
Work 8(6,4) rows without shaping. RC 324(338,352).

Shape shoulders:

Set machine to Hold.
At the opposite end to the carriage, the shoulder edge, put 5 needles to HP on next and every following alternate row × 6.
Knit 1 row over all needles then finish with waste yarn.
Remove from the machine.
Bring the 50(53,56) sts. back into work for the other side.
Set the card to the pattern row.
Lock card and move the carriage across without knitting and select the needles for the first pattern row.
Release card and work as given for the first side, reversing the shaping.
Finish on waste yarn.
Knit the remaining centre stitches off on to waste yarn.

Sleeves

Knit two alike.
Cast on over 65(68,71) needles for 2 × 1 mock rib.
Work as given for back welt. Inc 1(0,1) st and work joining row at MT + 2. Set machine for pattern.
RC 000. Inc 1 st each end of next and every following 8th row until there are 116(124,134) sts.
Work straight to RC 258(268,276).

Shape sleeve head:

Cast off 8(8,9) sts at beginning of next 2 rows.
Cast off 4 sts at the beginning of next 2 rows.
Dec 1 st each end of next and every following alternate row × 6. Knit 12(6,6) rows.
Dec 1 st each end of next and every following 4th row × 8(8,10).
Dec 1 st each end of next and every following alternate row × 3(6,6).
Dec 1 st each end of next and following row.
Dec 2 sts at each end of next 4 rows.
Cast off remaining 38(40,44) sts. RC 330(340,356).

Neckband

Join one shoulder seam.
With outside (purl side) facing pick up 48(50,52) sts from the centre back and

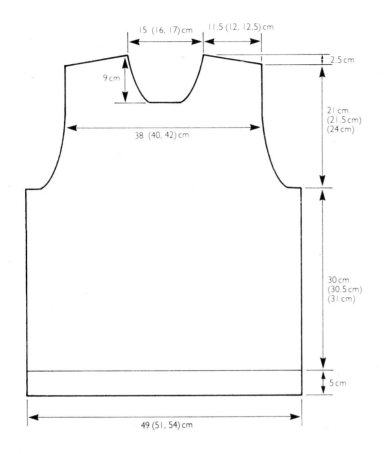

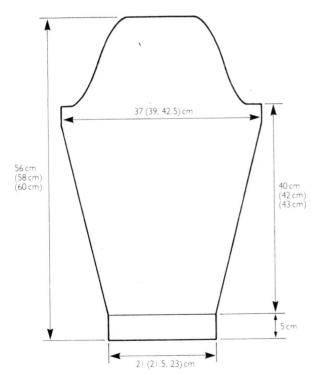

Slip Stitch Jumper with Set-In Sleeves:
Sizes 34 (36, 38) in chest/Sizes 86 (91, 97) cm chest

place them on to the machine.
Pick up 27 sts from the first side of front neck, 20 sts on waste yarn and 27 sts from the second side of the front neck. 74 sts.
Knit 1 row at MT. Knit 18 rows at MT − 2, 1 row MT + 2, 18 rows MT − 2 and 1 row MT.
Finish with waste yarn. Remove from machine.

Making up

Join remaining shoulder and neckband seam. Sew in sleeves. Stitch side and sleeve seams. Fold the neckband to the outside (the purl side) of the garment and backstitch into place.

Designing your own Set-in-Sleeve Jumper

See 'Taking Measurements' on pp. 115–117.

FAIR ISLE

(Also called Jacquard)

Uses

1. To knit different colours to make patterned shapes. Two colours are knitted in one row. The fabric is mostly used with the knit side outside.
2. To make a thick fabric by knitting from two cones of the same colour yarn.

Fair Isle is very quickly knitted on modern punchcard and electronic machines. On basic machines it can be worked by manual selection but, as each colour has to be knitted separately into the row it is time-consuming and only worth while if a small area of pattern is to be worked.

Unlike hand knitting, where the colour not being used is woven in as you knit, the knitting machine leaves the yarn free as floats. Long floats can be a nuisance when the garment is worn and should be avoided, particularly in children's garments.

DEALING WITH FLOATS

One way of overcoming the problem is to secure the floats by either latching them up, darning them in or lining the garment. Some proprietary treatments are available which fix the floats to the fabric but some of these require the use of a hot iron, which means they will be unsuitable for use with some yarns.

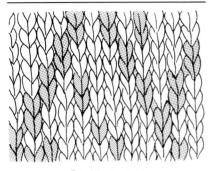

Fair Isle: *knit side.*

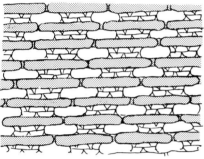

Fair Isle: *purl side.*

Methods

Latching up:

Using the latch tool, catch the lowest thread. Work a chain stitch up the fabric pulling the long floats through, sewing the last chain to the garment. This can also be done while the garment is being knitted on the machine, then the last chain is hung on to a needle, preferably one with a stitch of the same colour already on it. Take care not to pull the floats too tight as this makes the knit side of the pattern become distorted.

Darning:

Running stitches are made across the floats so that they are held against the knitting. Care must be taken that the stitches do not show on the knit side.

Lining:

This can be done either by using a manufactured knitted fabric which is especially made for knitwear and is pressed in place with a hot iron (not suitable for all yarns) or by knitting a lining with a fine yarn which is then sewn into place.

TIP

□ *When making your own card for a Fair Isle pattern, some floats can be reduced in length by adding smaller patterns as a background.*

Opposite: *Fair Isle samples (stitch patterns pp. 92–3); snow flake from Toyota 901 card 8.*

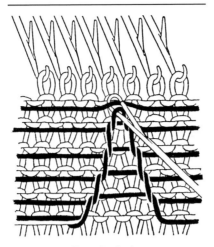

Floats latched up.
Avoid floats pulling too tight.

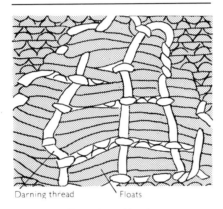

Darning thread   Floats

Floats darned in place.

KNITTING FAIR ISLE

Punchcard: Choose one of the cards from the standard pack which is suggested by the manufacturer for Fair Isle.

Put the card into the machine and lock on the first row.

Cast on with MY and knit a few rows. Set the machine to read the pattern and work 1 row. Thread in the 2nd colour and set the carriage for colour knitting: Knitmaster F, Brother MC, Toyota Colour and Singer Colour.

Release the card and continue knitting. You may find you need a larger stitch size than the one used for stocking stitch to produce the same tension. Toyota have a third tension wire which is clipped on to the tension wire carrying the second colour. The third tension wire on the Brother machine is used as an extra guide in the yarn threading. Both these devices give a tighter tension to the second yarn where required.

Practice

1. Try different punchcards.
2. Try different colours.
3. Try different yarns, including a thick and thin yarn used in the same card.

Notice that the size and shape of the pattern on the punch card is not always quite the same as the finished knitted pattern, therefore be prepared to experiment.

POSITIONING WITH 24 STITCH REPEAT

For positioning of Fair Isle patterns with 24 stitch repeat, the centre of the punchcard is the centre of the pattern and is knitted over the 12 needles either side of O. A pattern design having an odd number of stitches is centred on the first needle to the right of O.

To make a complete pattern at the side seam of a garment make sure that each edge of the front and back has half the pattern design + 1 stitch, or a complete pattern + 1 stitch. If this makes the garment too wide or too narrow move the knitting to one side of the centre O so that the central pattern design is in the centre of the finished knitting. (The extra stitch is used in sewing up.)

For example: If there are 6 pattern repeats each over 24 needles, then you would use 144 needles, arranged 72 at LHS and 72 at RHS of O, therefore making half a pattern at each edge of the knitting which can be matched when sewn up. If only 132 stitches are required to produce the finished width, then only $5\frac{1}{2}$ pattern repeats in all would be knitted. $5\frac{1}{2}$ repeats worked over the needle bed, with the same number of needles either side of O, will give only one quarter of a repeat at each side edge. To avoid this the needles can be arranged with 60 at LHS and 72 at RHS on the garment front and 72 at LHS and 60 at RHS on the back, giving one half of a pattern repeat at one side only on each piece. These sewn together will give a whole pattern. Remember that 1 extra stitch is needed at each side for sewing up the seam.

POSITIONING WITH OTHER THAN 24 STITCH PATTERNS

For positioning of Fair Isle patterns with stitch pattern repeats of 12, 8, etc, use the same method as above based on your stitch pattern repeat figures.

Needle arrangement
120 needles, but only 84 needles required

LHS					RHS		
60	36	12		12	36	60	

Side seam join

Side seam join

Side seam

84 needles used to knit front

Side seam

Side seam

84 needles used to knit back

Fair Isle: pattern positioning with a 24-stitch repeat. Useful for border patterns.

V NECK SHAPING

The depth of the V on the front (or back) of a garment is a matter of personal choice, influenced by fashion and style. The V is made by decreasing at the centre front (or back) of the garment. One side is worked at a time.

A V neck on a sideways knitted garment can be shaped by using the holding technique. The stitches to be used for the V neckband are put into HP then knitted on waste yarn with a central row of nylon cord and finished with waste yarn. The second side is shaped by returning stitches to WP. On completion of the knitting the nylon cord is removed and the V edge stitches held by waste yarn are picked up to knit the neckband.

TIP
□ *To make a neat join knit the front of the garment with an odd number of stitches, then when dividing for the neck put the central stitch on to a safety pin. Knit the two sides of the V neck and the neckbands, then finish the centre join by picking up the stitch from the safety pin and working a chain stitch over the central join.*

NECKBANDS

The shaping of the band is made at the point of the V. Because the shaping of the V is at the centre most bands knitted on to the garment are in two sections joined both at the V and either the shoulder seam or centre back. Bands sewn on to the garment are knitted in one piece and joined at the V. It is possible to knit a band in one length and then join it to the garment by knitting, but because the neck opening will not stretch the length of the stitches, it has to be joined in two sections, casting off each section separately.

VARIATIONS IN THE CENTRE OF V NECKBAND SHAPING

Band 1: The easiest V shaping is knitted without working any shaping at all to the ends. The straight ends are overlapped and sewn down.

Band 2: An alternative is to work no shaping at the ends of the band but, instead of overlapping them, sew along the centre line of the V the remaining flaps folded back and sewn behind the band.

Band 3: Shaped ends are made by decreasing and increasing, then sewing the shaped edges together.

Band 4: Placing needles in HP can be used to shape the ends of the band.

Practice

First knit the main front and back sections on which to try out the bands.

Use 4 ply for a standard gauge machine [DK for a chunky].

Back

Work a closed edge cast on over 56 [38] sts.
Knit 60 [40] rows stocking stitch.
Shape shoulder by putting 6 sts to HP at alternate ends on the next 6 [4] rows.
Knit back and shoulders off separately on to waste yarn.

Front

Cast on as for back. Knit to RC 034 [022].
Put 28 [19] needles at LHS to HP. (Or knit them back to NWP on nylon cord.) See also p. 69.
RC 000. Knit 1 row on needles at RHS.
Dec 1 st at neck edge on next and every alternate row x 10 [7], then knit to RC 025 [017].
Shape shoulder by putting 6 needles to HP at armhole edge on next and following alternate rows x 3 [2].
Finish on waste yarn.
Return needles at LHS to WP and work as for RHS reversing shapings.
Finish on waste yarn and join one shoulder.

Neckband

To work neckband directly on to the garment use one of the following methods.

Unshaped V bands:
Bands 1 and 2: With the inside of the garment facing, estimate the number of needles by holding the edge to the machine without stretching the fabric, pick up neck edge stitches with the 3-pronged transfer tool and hook them on to the needles.
Work on one side of the V first (the side which is not joined at the shoulder).
Thread in the main yarn and knit 1 row at MT + 1.
If a 1 x 1 or 2 x 1 mock rib band is required, arrange the needles before working the rest of the band.
Knit 12 [8] rows MT − 2, 1 row MT + 2, 12 [8] rows MT − 2.
Finish with waste yarn.
Knit the 2nd side of the band by picking up the same number of stitches as the first side of the V, and the stitches from the back of the garment and 1 extra needle at the shoulder edge for sewing the band together.
Knit the band as given for the first side

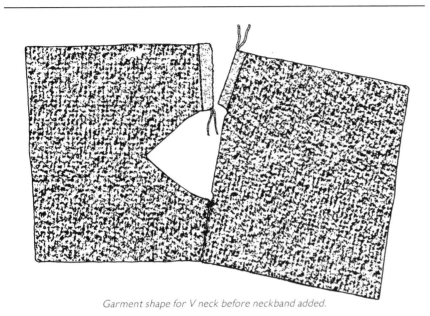

Garment shape for V neck before neckband added.

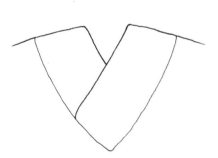

V neckband shaping:
inside view of Band 1.

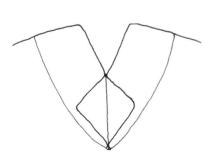

V neckband shaping:
inside view of Band 2.

and finish on waste yarn.
Join the 2nd shoulder seam.
Join the edges of the band at the shoulder point, then fold over the neckband and slip stitch the last row of the MY band to the inside of the garment. The V point ends are sewn down either as for Band 1 or Band 2.

Knitting Bands with V shaped ends on to garments:
The bands are picked up as before but the ends at the V point are shaped.

Band 3: Pick up the edge of one side of the V.
Knit 1 row MT + 1.
Using MT − 2, dec 1 st at the V shaped end on next and every following row until 12 [8] rows have been worked. Work 1 row MT + 2. MT − 2 inc 1 st at V shaped end on next and every following row until 25 [17] rows have been

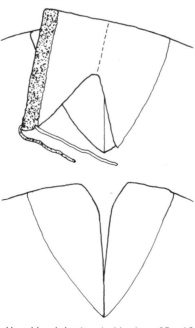

V neckband shaping: *inside view of Band 3. Join shaped edges first.*

worked altogether. Finish with waste yarn. Work the 2nd side and back in the same way, shaping at the V as before. Sew down to finish.

Band 4: Instead of increasing and decreasing at the V, the needles are put into HP and the carriage set to Hold. As the 2nd section of the band is knitted the needles are returned to UWP and knitted back to WP. Both bands are sewn into place and joined at the shoulder.

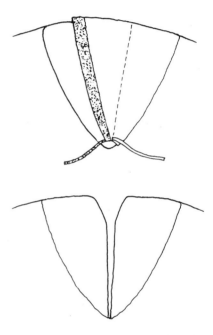

V neckband shaping: *inside view of Band 4.*

Bands knitted separately:
The band is knitted as though knitting a hem or rib. It is very often easier to knit it in two sections if joining it on to the garment neck using the machine. Work the first section at either the length of the V or the length of the V + half of the back neck stitches. Calculate the number of stitches required and cast on with waste yarn. Knit 6–8 rows then 1 row with nylon cord.
Using MY and working shaping if required, knit 12 [8] rows MT − 2. Knit 1 row MT + 2 and 12 [8] rows MT − 2. Turn up band. Knit 1 row MT + 1. Remove nylon cord and waste yarn. Take the V neck of the garment with the inside facing and hook the edge on to the needles already carrying stitches. Knit 1 row at a loose tension cast off. Work the other side in the same way but work the shaping, if required, at the other end of the band. Join the ends of the V band.

Above: *V neck shaping: small scale sample neckbands. (From top) Band 1, Band 2, Band 3, Band 4. (See p. 88).*
Right: *Alternative stitch pattern for V neck Fair Isle slipover knitted in 4 colours (stitch pattern p. 93).*

Bands can be knitted and finished on
waste yarn and then stitched to the
garment.

TIP
□ *If you find that the band you have
knitted will not lie flat or is stretching
the neck opening try again with fewer
stitches. Even where written pattern
instructions give you the number of
stitches needed to knit a band, you may
not like the finished result. It is worth
re-knitting until you are satisfied. If you
want to hold the centre back stitches,
use a knitting needle to pick up and
hold the stitches unravelled from the
band.*

V NECK SLIPOVER

This is knitted in a Fair Isle pattern over
a 12 stitch pattern repeat with short
floats. The neckband has shaped ends
using the holding method and is knitted
in stocking stitch. (Photos pp. 26–7,
46–7.)

Sizes: 34(36,38,40,42) in/
86(91,97,102,107) cm chest/bust.

Yarn: 4 ply acrylic MY 250 g, second colour 150 g.

Tension: 32 sts and 35 rows to 10 cm
square.

Stitch pattern:

○ main yarn (MY)
● 2nd colour

Back
Cast on with waste yarn over
153(161,171,179,187) needles for 1 x 1
mock rib welt. Knit 6–8 rows. Work 1
row with nylon cord.
Thread MY. Knit 20 rows MT − 2, 1
turning row MT + 2, 20 rows MT − 2.

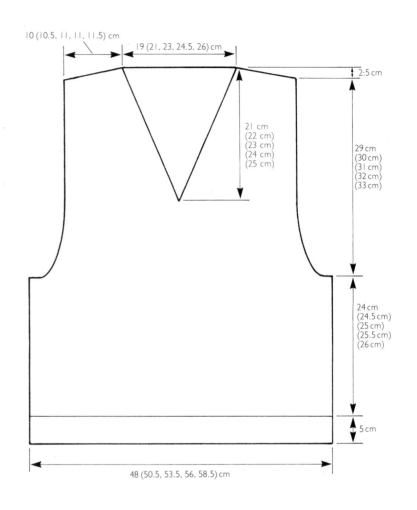

V Neck Slipover:
Sizes 34 (36, 38, 40, 42) in chest/Sizes 86 (91, 97, 102, 107) cm chest

Pick up welt. Set machine to pattern.
Knit 1 row MT + 1.
RC 000. Set machine to knit colour.
Thread in 2nd colour. MT. Knit to RC
84(86,88,90,92).

Shape armholes:
Cast off 8 sts at the beginning of the
next 2 rows.
Cast off 2 sts at the beginning of the
next 2 rows.
Dec 1 st each end on next and every alternate row x 4.
Stitches remaining
125(133,143,151,159).
Work straight to RC
186(190,196,202,208).

Shape shoulder:
Set carriage to Hold. At the opposite
end to the carriage put 8 sts to HP on
the next and following 6 rows, then
8(9,11,12,13) sts to HP on the next 2
rows. Cancel Hold setting and knit 1

row plain in MY over all the needles.
Knit shoulder sts on to waste yarn,
working one side at a time. Knit the
back neck 61(67,73,79,85) sts on to
waste yarn.

V neck front
Work as back to RC
112(112,116,118,120).
(The armhole shaping has been
worked.)
Place the centre stitch on to a length of
waste yarn or a safety pin. Record pattern row number and RC reading.
Work over the 62(66,71,75,79) sts at
one side.
Work 1 row.
Dec 1 st at neck edge on next and every
following alternate row
x 30(33,36,39,42) until 32(33,35,36,37)
sts remain.
Work straight to RC
186(190,196,202,208).

Shape shoulder

RHS of garment, work 1 row before shaping shoulder.

Work as given for back, putting the needles into HP at the opposite end to the carriage at the armhole edge on every alternate row. Knit 1 row plain and finish with waste yarn.

Return the stitches on the second side to WP.

Set the pattern card to the recorded row and move the carriage one row to select the pattern without knitting. Set RC to reading from start of first side.

Shape the 2nd side in the same way as the first, but reversing the shaping. Finish with waste yarn.

Neckband

Join one shoulder. Estimate the number of stitches needed for the neckband. Try the short side first, i.e. one side of the V without the back neck stitches. Cast on with waste yarn and knit 6–8 rows then 1 row with the nylon cord. Using MY, knit 1 row MT. Set carriage to Hold.

Bring 1 needle to HP at the end of the knitting which is to be the centre of the V. To find which end this is take the front of the garment with the inside facing you and put it up to the knitting. The end to be shaped will depend on which shoulder seam has been joined. MT − 2. Knit 1 row and bring a 2nd needle to HP at the V point end. Repeat this until 11 rows in all have been worked and there are 10 needles in HP. Knit 1 row MT + 2.

On the next and every following row, push 1 needle back to UWP until all needles are back in work. Knit 1 row MT.

Pick up stitches to make a hem and knit 1 row MT + 1.

With inside (purl side) of front facing, hook the neck edge on to the needles already carrying stitches. Work 1 row and cast off loosely.

Repeat for the second side and back neck stitches. Join second shoulder. To finish the neckband, take the centre front stitch and chain stitch up over the joined shaped neckband.

Armbands

These are worked in the same way as the neckband and joined at the under arm seam.

Making up

Join side seams.

SLIPOVER IN FOUR COLOURS

Below is the pattern for the slipover shown on the back cover – easy to knit with your own combination of colours. The pattern colour is changed after 2 rows have been knitted in background colour only. This makes it easy to see the point at which you change the colour. It is easier if the pattern colour is removed from the carriage before knitting the 2 background colour rows. There is no need to break the yarn between the blocks of colour, just make sure when changing the colour that the yarn is held at the end of the previous block of the same colour and is not pulled up to the knitting. Placing your finger between the edge of the knitting and the thread will give enough 'free' yarn and prevent the yarn pulling. See p. 92 to drawn your own pattern.

SINGLE MOTIF KNITTING

A single motif is a section of patterned knitting set in plain stocking stitch. It is usually Fair Isle but can also be tuck, slip or weaving. To make a single motif the machine is set to knit the stitch pattern over an isolated group of needles. Where no mechanism for knitting a single motif is available, but when knitting Fair Isle normally the patterning needles are selected to the UWP (Brother, Toyota and Singer), a single block of Fair Isle pattern can be worked by pushing the needles not required for the pattern to the WP on every row.

TIP
☐ *Where the letters of the alphabet are used on a punchcard machine, the card is usually punched out as a mirror-image. You can punch the holes so that the letter is the right way round, but reverse the punchcard when putting it in the machine. On the sheet for an electronic machine write the letter in the normal way but select the pattern reverse button 1.*

KNITTING FAIR ISLE SINGLE MOTIF

Refer to your instruction book and set the needle bed and carriage to knit a single motif.

It is usually worked over blocks of 24 stitches, the block in the centre being over 12 needles either side of the O.

Machines with a zig-zag patterning mechanism (Toyota), and electronic machines, can place the motif anywhere and are not restricted to the blocks of 24.

TIP
☐ *If your machine brings selected needles to UWP, before knitting try a 'dry run' to check that the pattern will be in the expected place.*

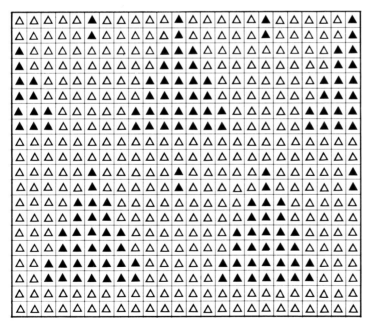

△ background colour   ▲ pattern colour

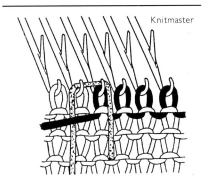

Knitmaster

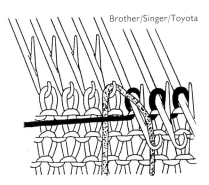

Brother/Singer/Toyota

Single motif: *binding to prevent edge gaps.*

When the second colour is introduced into the motif knitting, the side of the motif may be pulled in, making the pattern bulge and forming a ladder at the side. To avoid: weave in two lengths of spare yarn at the side of the knitting between the carriage and the motif, one edge on every other row.

Hang the length of yarn on to the last needle of the stitches knitted in the second colour and on to the adjacent needle carrying a stitch knitted in the background colour.

The carriage is moved across for the second row and the second length of yarn is used in the same way. When the third row is knitted the first length of yarn is picked up and hung over a needle with a stitch in the second colour and the adjacent main yarn stitch. This is repeated as the motif proceeds and the ends are darned in at the making-up stage.

Electronic machines: Use the reverse background switch and the main/background yarn in the second colour feed on the carriage. The motif can then be wrapped in the same way as when needles are in HP.

Opposite: *Knitting a single motif more than 24 stitches wide, the design is drawn on squared paper indicating the extra stitches to be selected manually.*

MOTIF WIDER THAN 24 STITCHES

To knit a motif which is wider than 24 stitches (or the number of stitches on your punchcard):
1. Work out the design on squared paper.
2. Transfer the centre of the pattern to a punchcard.
3. Set the machine to knit the punchcard and single motif.
4. The needles for the extra stitches of the design can be pulled out to HP or UWP and will knit in the motif yarn.

DESIGNING YOUR OWN V NECK PATTERN SLIPOVER

The basic shape already used for the front and back of the set-in sleeve jumper is used for the slipover pattern. (See measurement section pp. 115–117.) The armholes are drawn deeper and the shoulders narrower. Drop the armhole between 2 and 5 cm and re-draw the shaping curve. The shoulders need to be 2–4 cm narrower than for a set-in sleeve. Remember to allow for neck and armbands. The depth of the V is a matter of personal choice. Bands which finish 17 cm for a woman (36 in) and 21 cm for a man (40 in) below the neck point are about right for a V neck depth to show effectively on the garment in wear.

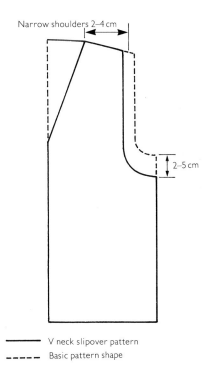

Narrow shoulders 2–4 cm

2–5 cm

——— V neck slipover pattern
- - - - Basic pattern shape

Designing your own V neck pattern slipover.

WEAVING

Weaving a second yarn in with the knitting yarn produces a fabric which is more stable and less elastic than any other knitted stitch pattern. Thick textured yarns that the machine will not normally knit can be woven. Less of the second colour yarn is used in weaving than in Fair Isle, therefore expensive yarns go further when woven. Weaving is always worked on the purl side of the knitting and this technique can be used on all machines, but weaving brushes are needed for 'automatic' weaving.

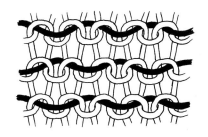

Weaving

MANUAL WEAVING

Manual weaving requires no weaving brushes. The weaving yarn is taken under and over needles in HP or UWP. When the carriage is moved across the MY knits over the weaving yarn. Patterns are made by selecting different needle arrangements, for example, every other needle or every 3rd needle with the weaving yarn placed over the first selected needle and under the second selected needle. The weaving yarn can also be wrapped round two or three needles several times to make a bobble effect. The weaving yarn can be used every row or every third row, or to form blocks of colour over part of a row.

AUTOMATIC WEAVING WITH WEAVING BRUSHES

Punchcard and electronic machines are fitted with weaving brushes, some earlier models have weaving brushes as an optional extra.

The yarn to be woven is laid across selected needles and, when the carriage moves across, the brushes push the yarn down over these needles. The new stitch is made over the weaving yarn so holding it in place. At the end of the row the yarn is moved to the side of the carriage nearest the needles ready to be laid in front of the selected needles on the next row.

Two methods of feeding the weaving yarn

1. Using the weaving yarn threaded through the tension arm.
2. Manually laying the weaving yarn across selected needles and controlling the tension by hand.

The most automatic method of weaving is that where a machine has a special weaving carriage attachment, as the one produced by Knitmaster. Here the weaving yarn from the tension mast is threaded into the special carriage and automatically transferred from one end of the carriage to the other as the knitting proceeds. The woven fabric is quickly knitted but the thickness of the yarn is limited as it must pass through the yarn tension discs. It must also be knitted on every row.

Machines without a weaving carriage can be used with the weaving yarn passing through the yarn tension discs. The carriage is set to pattern, the weaving brushes set into working position and the weaving yarn in place at the side of the carriage nearest the working needles. The carriage moves across and the yarn is woven into the knitting. The actual placement of the weaving yarn will be described in your instruction book. At the end of the row the weaving yarn is moved to the other side of the carriage for the next row. The advantage of this method is that the weaving yarn tension is controlled and not every row need have the weaving yarn included. Again yarns which do not run freely through the tension discs should be avoided.

Where the yarn is not threaded through the tension mast, the cone of weaving yarn is placed in front of the machine. A machine where needles are selected to the UWP is best for this method. (Machines where the needles remain in WP can be used but the needles have to be placed in HP manually which is time-consuming.)

After securing the free end, the weaving yarn is laid across the selected needles. As the carriage moves across, knitting in the weaving yarn, the tension is controlled by hand. At the end of the row the weaving yarn is brought round under the carriage and over the selected needles again. This may seem a slow method but it is possible to establish a working rhythm which allows the knitting to proceed quickly. This method has the advantage that thicker and textured knobbly yarns can be woven.

Manual weaving: *weaving yarn taken under and over pattern needles in* HP.

Practice

1. Use cards and patterns suggested in your instruction book.
2. Knit random blocks of weaving or occasional rows.
3. Use different thicknesses of yarn.
4. Decoration by making bobbles, cutting weaving strands and latching up weaving strands from a few rows below.

WOVEN JACKET

This jacket is knitted sideways. This means that the starting row is down the centre front and the knitting continues round the body, with shaping, to finish at the centre front. There are no side seams and the shoulders are sewn. The sleeves are knitted sideways and the underarm seam is closed using the sewing machine and cut to shape or can be knitted to shape using the holding technique. Try making the armholes deeper and make a sleeveless waistcoat. The neck, hem and cuffs, or armholes if making a waistcoat, are trimmed with a bias knitted strip. Pockets are sewn in place.

New techniques for the woven jacket are: knitting sideways, bias strips, patch pockets.

KNITTING THE WOVEN JACKET

Sizes: 38(40,42) in/97(102,107) cm chest/bust.

Yarn: 400 g 4 ply acrylic as MY + 300 g 4 ply acrylic used double for the weaving yarn.

Tension: 23 sts and 37 rows to 10 cm.

Stitch pattern:

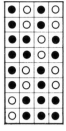

○ blanks – stitch knits over weaving yarn
● holes – yarn free/float

Patterned notes

1. All shaping on main part of garment is at LHS of knitting.
2. The garment is started at the centre front. To make the stitch pattern easier to work, the knitting is started on waste yarn and the nylon cord is then used to separate the waste yarn from the main 'e-wrap' cast-on edge.
3. The garment is worked in MT throughout.

Method: To knit the jacket

Push to WP 50(52,54) needles at LHS of centre O and 74(76,78) needles at RHS of centre O.

Using waste yarn, work an open edge cast on. Knit 6–8 rows. Carriage at LHS. Knit I row with nylon cord.

With MY work 'e-wrap' cast on. Thread MY into carriage.

Knit I row. Feed in card. Lock on row I.

Set machine to pattern. Knit I row. Set weaving brushes into working position and commence pattern knitting.

Release card. Set RC to 000. Work 13(15,17) rows in pattern.

At LHS of work inc I st on next and following 4th row, then inc I st on following 5th row.

Inc I st on every following alternate row x 5.

Inc I st at LHS on next row. Knit I row.

Cast on 5 sts at beginning of next, then 10 sts at beginning of following alternate row. 148(152,156) sts.

RC 38(40,42).

First shoulder slope:

Dec I st on 5th and every following 5th row until 140(144,148) sts remain. Knit straight to RC 81(85,89).

First armhole:

At LHS cast of 52(53,54) sts. Knit I row.

Dec I st at LHS on next and every following row x 7 in all. Knit to RC 109(113,117).

Inc I st at LHS on next and every following row × 7.
Knit I row.
At LHS Cast on ('e' wrap) 52(53,54) sts.
Knit 4(6,8) rows.
Inc I st at LHS on next and every following 5th row until there are

148(152,156) sts.
Work to RC 161(167,173).

Back neck:
At LHS dec I st at beginning of next and every following alternate row × 3.
Work straight to RC 231(241,253). Inc I

st at LHS on next and every following alternate row × 3.

Second shoulder slope:
Dec I st at LHS on the 5th and every following 5th row to until 140(144,148) sts remain.
Work to RC 275(287,301).

Second armhole:
At LHS cast off 52(53,54) sts. Knit I row. Dec I st at LHS on next and every following row × 7 in all. Knit 20 rows.
Inc I st at LHS on next and every following row × 7. Knit I row. RC 311(323,337).
At LHS cast on 52(53,54) sts. Knit 4(6,8) rows. Inc I st at LHS on next and every following 5th row until there are 148(152,156) sts.
Work to RC 355(369,385).

Front neck:
At LHS cast off 10 sts and knit 2 rows.
Cast off 5 sts and knit 2 rows.
Dec I st at LHS on next and following row, then dec I st at LHS on every alternate row × 5.
At LHS dec I st on 4th and following 4th row. Knit 13(15,17) rows. Knit I row in MY only. Cast off.

SLEEVES

Methods
Either
Knit 2 pieces of fabric 124(126,128) sts × 188(192,196) rows and shape them according to the measurements on the diagram. Tack the lines to be sewn on to fabric. Machine stitch using I × I (I mm × I mm) zig-zag swing stitch. Cut to shape, then sew in place.
or
Knit a shaped sleeve 'sideways' from seam round to seam. The stitches are held in HP to shape the underarm. Automatic wrapping of yarn round the needles in HP is used in these instructions.

Cast on with waste yarn over 120(122,124) needles. Knit 6–8 rows. Knit I row with nylon cord. Carriage at LHS. Set carriage to read pattern with card locked on row I.
Thread MY. Knit I row. Push weaving brushes into working position and start knitting in pattern.
RC 000. Release card. Pattern 2 rows. Set carriage to Hold.
Carriage at RHS, RC 002. At RHS inc I st on this and every following 4th row until 124(126,128) needles are carrying stitches, AT THE SAME TIME at RC 002 put 106 needles at LHS to HP. Knit I row. Take yarns under first needle in HP
cont.

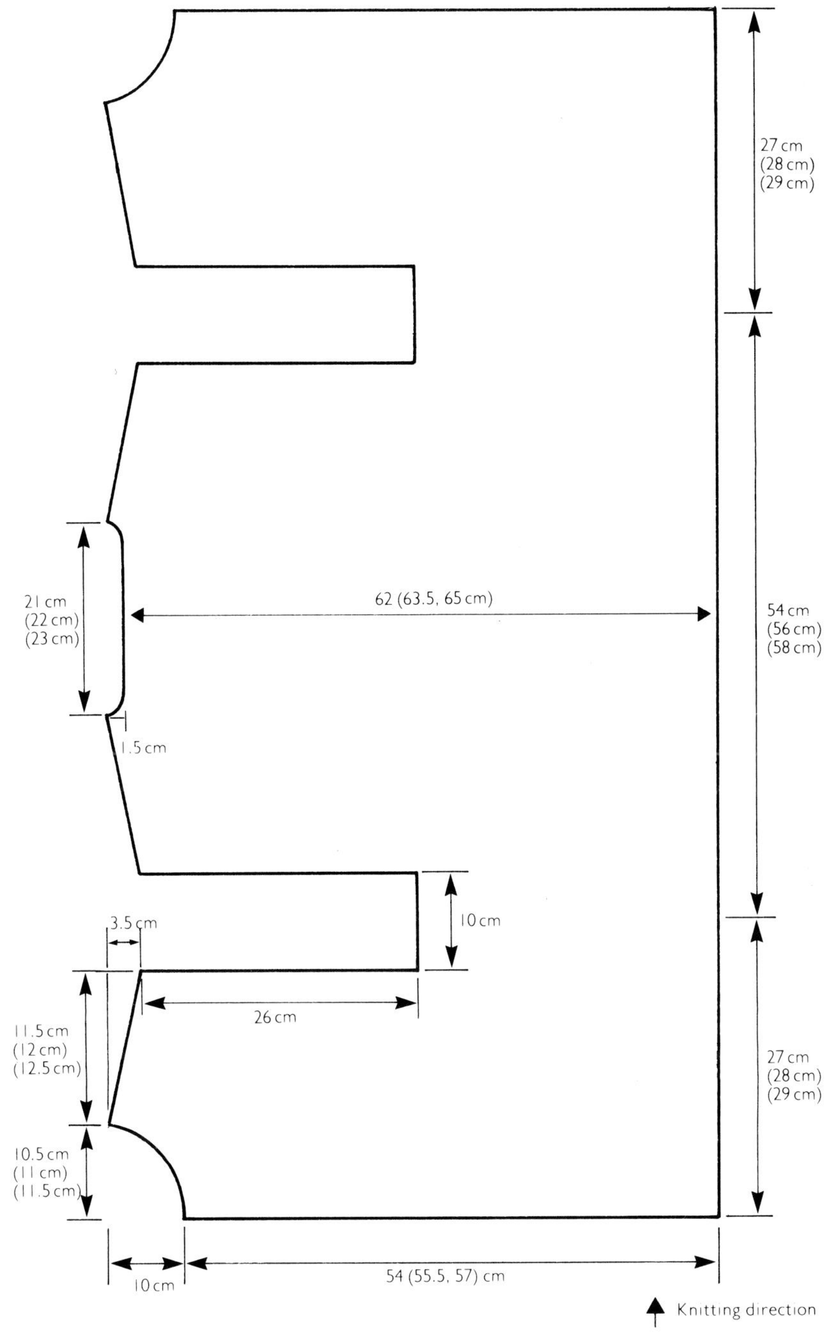

Woven jacket: *Sizes 38 (40, 42) in chest / Sizes 97 (102, 107) cm chest. For sleeves see p. 100*

Dimensions on diagram:
27 cm (28 cm) (29 cm)
21 cm (22 cm) (23 cm)
62 (63.5, 65 cm)
54 cm (56 cm) (58 cm)
1.5 cm
10 cm
3.5 cm
26 cm
11.5 cm (12 cm) (12.5 cm)
10.5 cm (11 cm) (11.5 cm)
27 cm (28 cm) (29 cm)
10 cm
54 (55.5, 57) cm
↑ Knitting direction

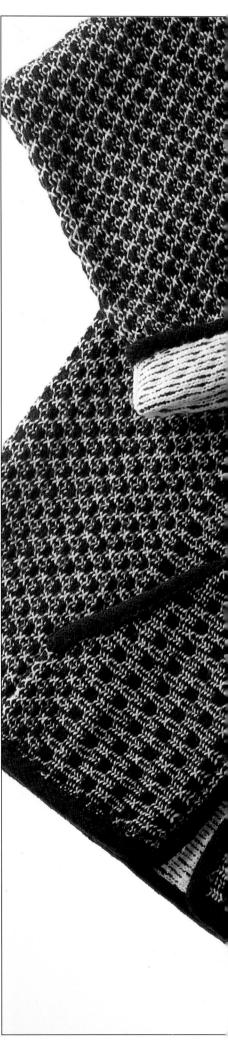

Above: *Weaving samples. (From top) Jacket pattern knitted in white on black, (author's design, stitch pattern p. 96); 2 colour silky ribbon changed every 4 rows Knitmaster card 3 (stitch pattern p. 72, col. 3); 4 colours laid on manually, card 1, (stitch pattern p. 72, col. 1).*
Right: *The woven jacket (pp. 96–100) knitted in 4 ply acrylic, with knitted bias trim and patch pockets (stitch pattern p. 96).* **Note:** *front and centre back panel patterns elongated.*

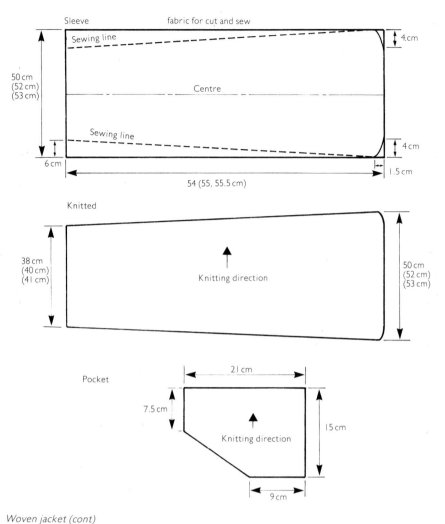

Woven jacket (cont)

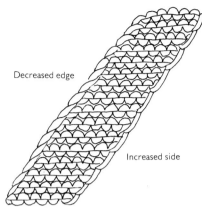

Bias strip: *purl side facing.*

BIAS STRIP

To calculate the tension for the strip:
1. At LHS of machine cast on with 'e-wrap' over 15 needles. Knit 2 rows.
2. Decrease 1 stitch at LHS and increase 1 st at RHS. Knit 2 rows.
Repeat step 2 for 20 rows. Cast off and remove strip from the machine. Half the width of the fabric will be the depth of the binding that will show. The strip will have to be sewn into place on both sides so decide how wide you require your strip. The length of 22 rows will serve as a guide to the length needed.

When you are knitting the strip itself and have worked across the whole of the needle bed of the machine transfer all the stitches back to the LHS and continue until you have knitted the required number of rows.

Making up

Sew shoulder seams. Sew in sleeves. Knit length of bias strip and sew in place round jackets edges, sleeve ends and pocket openings. Sew pockets in place.

DESIGNING YOUR OWN PATTERN

Extra ease is added to the jumper pattern measurements. The sideways knitting is useful for larger sizes, because when a garment is started at the centre front the only limitation is the number of needles needed to give a chosen back length. (*See chart opposite.*)

This jacket has a shallow sleeve head. The top of the sleeve is set into the armhole and sewn to the straight edge of the underarm section of the garment. Remember to check that the bottom of the jacket will go round the hips. Side vents can be worked if extra ease is preferred.

Knit 1 row.
Bring 10 needles at LHS to UWP from HP. Weave in weaving yarn by hand. Knit 1 row. Wrap yarns under first needle now in HP. Knit 1 row. Repeat these 2 rows until 6 sts remain in HP. Cancel Hold setting. Knit straight to RC 162(166,170).
Carriage at RHS. Set carriage to Hold. At LHS put 5 needles to HP. Knit 1 row. Bring 1 needle at LHS from WP to HP. Knit across. (You will see that the yarn has been automatically wrapped.).
* At LHS bring 9 needles to HP, knit 1 row, bring 1 needle to HP. Repeat from * until 14(16,18) needles remain in work, AT THE SAME TIME at RC 172(176,180), shaping is made at the RHS of work by dec 1 st at this end of the row and every 4th row until 14(16,18) sts remain in WP. Cancel Hold setting.
Work 2 rows in pattern. Cancel pattern.
Cast off 7 sts at RHS.

Join seam

Take the cast-on edge up and pick up the MY loops between the stitches knitted in nylon cord and hang them on to the corresponding needles with stitches and 7 needles for the armhole edge which will be cast off singly, i.e. not joined to the other side of the sleeve. Work 1 row with a large stitch size and cast off.

Pockets

Knit 2, reversing the shaping for the second pocket.
Cast on 20 sts with waste yarn. Knit 6–8 rows then 1 row with nylon cord. With MY 'e-wrap' cast on over nylon cord. Thread carriage. MT. Set the carriage and card for patterning. Knit 1 row. Set weaving brushes and knit the pattern. Inc 1 st at one end of the first and every following row until there are 48 stitches. Knit straight for 28 rows. Cancel pattern. Knit 1 row in MY (MT + 2). Cast off loosely.

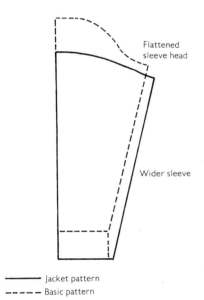

32–33 cm

Allowance for front band 0.5 cm   Add 2–4 cm

Flattened
sleeve head

Wider sleeve

——— Jacket pattern
– – – – Basic pattern

Designing your own woven jacket.

EXTRA EASE

Chest	5–10 cm
Armhole depth	2–4 cm
Upper arm	4–6 cm

LACE

Lace is a decorative stitch pattern producing an open work fabric. There are several types of lace stitches, some of which can be made on all machines.

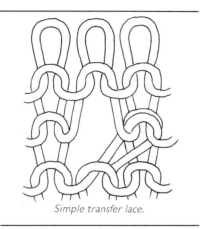

Simple transfer lace.

TRANSFER LACE

This is a pattern of holes made by transferring stitches. There are three methods of knitting transfer lace.

Simple lace

Two stitches are knitted together to make an adjacent hole.

Multi-transfer or Fashion lace

Two or three stitches are knitted together with the hole several stitches away.

Fine lace

This is a simple lace where the transferred stitch is partly retained on its original needle. The holes are smaller than those made by normal simple lace (Brother machines).

TRANSFER LACE KNITTING

Simple lace can be knitted on all machines by manually transferring a stitch to the adjacent needle. The empty needle is left in WP and a new stitch formed when the carriage is moved across the needle bed.

TIP
□ To avoid forming a bias, where the fabric twists to a diamond shape rather than an oblong, transfer the stitches in alternate directions. On one row transfer to the left, the next to the right. The tension of a lacy fabric is similar to that of stocking stitch.

AUTOMATIC TRANSFER LACE KNITTING

This is an area where there is the greatest difference between manufacturers' methods.

With previous stitch patterns it has been possible to interchange patterns, provided simple rules were observed. Lace knitting is different for each make of machine. Most of the machines knit lace stitch patterns with the use of a separate carriage, but the Toyota 950 has the lace knitting facility built in the main carriage.

The Knitmaster lace carriage selects, transfers and knits stitches on one row for simple lace, though fashion lace requires the yarn to be removed from the carriage in order to move the stitches first without knitting.

Brother, Singer (Superba) and Toyota (except the 950) machines have a lace carriage which reads the pattern and selects needles to the UWP but does not carry the yarn. The main carriage carries the yarn and knits two plain rows between movements of the lace carriage. Whichever carriage is not working rests on extension rails fitted at either end of the needle bed. Combination stitch patterns may be knitted where both carriages pattern, for example, tuck and lace or lace and weaving.

Because of the differences in the lace pattern mechanisms, the punchcards also differ. The same stitch pattern cannot necessarily be made on a different make of machine. Lace pattern punchcards supplied with your machine in the standard pack will enable you to try lace, and most manufacturers also produce additional cards.

TIP
□ In the stitch transfer process, the needles are pushed over the adjacent needles. This is noisy and quite alarming at first, but it is a normal process. The needles are designed to withstand this movement.

KNITTING A TRANSFER LACE PATTERN

Use a slightly larger stitch size than the stocking stitch MT you would use for the same yarn and hang on additional weights. Try, at first, knitting with a soft, non-springy yarn.

For Knitmaster

Use the lace carriage only. Set the carriage to read the pattern. Lock the card on the first row. Move the carriage across the stitches, then release the card and knit across. The needles are selected, the stitches transferred and then the row knitted all in the one

Above: *A selection of lace samples. (From top) fine lace (Brother 910, sheet 10, pattern 34); fashion or multi-transfer lace; punch or thread lace (author's design); tuck lace (Chunky machine); for simple lace see the photograph on pp. 118–119).*
Right: *V neck lacy cotton top. The armhole edge can be crocheted or finished with a band (stitch pattern Brother Electronic 910, sheet 10, taken from pattern 34).*

movement of the carriage. For fashion lace the punchcard is marked where the yarn is removed and then replaced, in order to transfer stitches, without knitting.

For the Brother, Toyota, Singer Superba

The main carriage remains on the needle bed and the lace carriage is placed at the LHS, the opposite end to the main carriage. Lock the card on the first row and move the lace carriage across. Release the card. Move the lace carriage back to the LHS. Needles that were selected in the first move will be transferred. Knit two rows with the main carriage. If more needles are selected when the lace carriage is moved to the LHS, continue moving this carriage to and fro across the needle bed until, with the lace carriage at the LHS, no more needles are selected.

Check the pattern card (or row window on the Brother 950) and read the number of rows of plain knitting with the main carriage. This is usually 2 rows, but more can be worked if you wish the lacy pattern to have wider bands of plain knitting between repeats. The row counter is operated only by the main carriage. Multi-transfer moves made by the lace carriage do not register and are therefore not included.

To avoid end stitches dropping
For the Knitmaster: Put in end stoppers.

For the Brother, Toyota, Singer:
Needles selected at either end should be pushed back from the UWP to WP.

Tip
□ *It is not possible to knit lace with needles in HP; therfore, stitches requiring to be held must be knitted back on nylon cord to NWP.*

Correcting lace patterns
1. Where the selected needles are brought to UWP by moving the lace carriage without knitting the 2 rows between the patterns: Push the needles back to WP, return the lace carriage to the LHS and re-set the card. Work the plain knit rows and continue knitting pattern.
2. If too many rows have been knitted and the stitches transferred, unravel the yarn or transfer the stitches back to a plain knit row. Care is needed when picking up stitches – it is often quicker to start again.

PUNCH OR THREAD LACE
This is a pattern knitted with a main yarn and a very fine yarn. The stitches are not transferred and the lace effect is made by the fine yarn being almost invisible. The fine yarn knits with the main yarn so there are no floats (Knitmaster machines and Brother 950).

TUCK LACE
This is another lacy effect fabric made by using the tuck stitch setting on the

carriage with selected needles left in NWP.

Owners of Brother machines may need to make an adjustment to the end needle selection mechanism when using this stitch or knit using the KC II setting. The instructions will be in the instruction manual.

V NECK LACY COTTON TOP

A loose fitting top knitted with a simple lace stitch pattern. The armhole edge is crocheted or finished with a band.

Size: One size only to fit 34–42 in.

Yarn: 250g Handywoman 3 ply cotton.

Tension: 30 sts and 40 rows to 10 cm square.

Lace Pattern: Any simple lace pattern.

Elastic for machine knitters
In order to retain the elasticity in the welt, a specially manufactured fine elastic thread is knitted into the underside of the welt. The elastic is threaded into the carriage with the main yarn and the tension is either controlled by threading through the tension arm or manually.

Knit the elastic for 2–4 rows at the beginning, middle and end of the underside of the welt. More than a few rows may produce a hard section of fabric with all the elasticity lost.

Back
Cast on for 1 x 1 mock rib over 175 sts. Knit with waste yarn and nylon cord. With MY knit 30 rows MT−2, working elastic if required, 1 row MT+1, 30 rows MT−2. Turn up hem. Knit 1 row MT+1.
RC 000. Work in pattern to RC 092. Inc 1 st each end of next and every following alternate row x 9. 193 sts.
Work in pattern, without shaping, to RC 212

Shape shoulders
At opposite end to carriage, knit 12 sts back to NWP on nylon cord on next and every following row x 12 in all. (49 sts remain in centre.)
Knit centre back stitches on waste yarn for 6–8 rows, break yarn and remove

Knit side of punch lace.

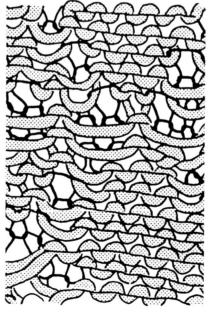

Purl side of punch lace.

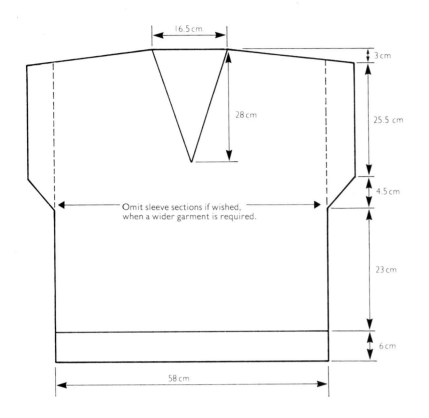

16.5 cm

3 cm

28 cm

25.5 cm

4.5 cm

Omit sleeve sections if wished,
when a wider garment is required.

23 cm

6 cm

58 cm

One Size Lacy Cotton Top: 34–42 in chest/85–106 cm chest.

stitches from needles. Push empty needles back to NWP. Bring one set of 72 needles back to WP, remove nylon cord from these needles and knit off on to waste yarn.
Repeat with second shoulder.

Front
Work as given for back to RC 112. Put the centre stitch on to a length of contrast yarn. Knit back to NWP 96 sts at one side of centre O, using nylon cord. Continue working in pattern on the remaining stitches.
Decrease 1 st at neck edge on next and every following 4th row until 24 decreases have been worked. 72 sts.
Work straight to RC 211.

Shape shoulder
(At RHS, work 1 more row before shaping shoulder.)
Knit 12 sts back to NWP on nylon cord at opposite end to carriage (the armhole edge) on every alternate row. Finish with waste yarn. Return the needles in NWP to WP, remove cord

and knit the 2nd side as given for first, reversing the shaping.

V Band
Join one shoulder and work V band of your own choice. To finish, join second shoulder and crochet or knit a band round the armhole edges. Sew side seams.

KNITTING YOUR OWN GARMENT

This is a very easy shape to knit. One limitation is the number of stitches required to give your designed width. It is possible to use the full needle bed for the main body then to add the sleeves afterwards. The shape can be knitted narrower and shorter, or longer as required. It is easy to knit this simple shape and so concentrate on the lace patterning.

RAGLAN STYLE SHAPING

Raglan shaping at the armhole edges produces a classic style garment, with an added advantage for those with wide or narrow shoulders in that the garment will fit well and be comfortable to wear. Raglan armholes are deeper than those for set-in sleeves, and sleeve length measurement is taken from the base of the neck over the edge of the shoulder to the wrist. This is basically the same length as an arm length, plus the shoulder. The shaping on the knitting can be emphasised by using a fully fashioned decrease.

RAGLAN CARDIGAN

This cardigan has picot edges added to the lower hem, cuffs, neckbands and pocket tops. The pockets are knitted on to the garment after the fronts have been completed.

Sizes: 36(38,40) in/91(97,102) cm chest/bust.

Yarn: 3 ply botany wool, or equivalent yarn. 300 g.

Tension: 34 sts and 46 rows to 10 cm.

Back
Cast on with waste yarn for 1 x 1 mock rib over 181(187,195) needles.
For hem knit 6–8 rows waste yarn and 1 row nylon cord. With MY, knit 9 rows MT − 1, 1 row MT + 1.
Bring needles in NWP forward to WP. RC 000. Knit 1 row MT + 1 over all working needles, then knit 9 rows MT − 1.
Join hem by picking up loops between nylon cord from first row of MY. Knit 1 row MT + 1.
MT. Knit to RC 160(164,166).

Shape armholes
Cast off 10 sts at beginning of next 2 rows.
Note: For fully fashioned shaping see p. 39. *cont.*

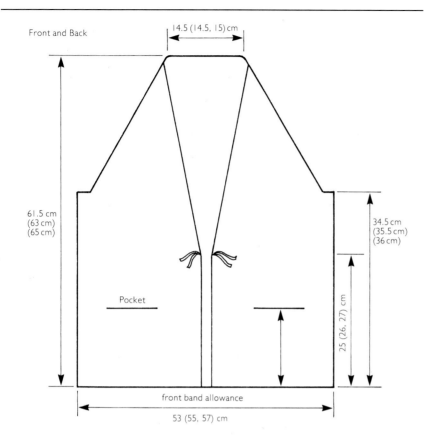

Front and Back

14.5 (14.5, 15) cm

61.5 cm
(63 cm)
(65 cm)

34.5 cm
(35.5 cm)
(36 cm)

Pocket

25 (26, 27) cm

front band allowance

53 (55, 57) cm

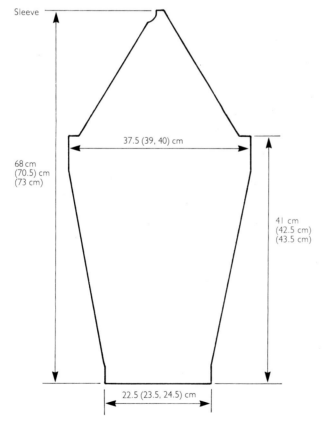

Sleeve

37.5 (39, 40) cm

68 cm
(70.5) cm
(73 cm)

41 cm
(42.5 cm)
(43.5 cm)

22.5 (23.5, 24.5) cm

Raglan style cardigan pattern measurements.

Hang claw weights to edges of work when shaping raglan seams.
Dec 2 sts at each end of next and every following 4th row × 28(29,31). RC 274(282,288).
2nd size only
Dec 1 st each end of following 4th row
All sizes
Knit to RC 280(290,300).
Knit remaining 49(49,51)sts on to waste yarn for 6–8 rows and remove from machine.

Right front

Cast on for 1 × 1 mock rib over 86(91,93) needles. (Bring an extra needle to WP where required.)
Work hem as given for back to RC 010.
Join hem (decreasing extra st if necessary).
Knit joining row at MT + 1. Knit to RC 016.

Mark outline of pocket:
(See also p. 113.)
Transfer 23rd(27th,28th) stitch from RHS of work and 20th(23rd,25th) stitch from LHS of work on to the adjacent needles.
Knit in a marker thread for base of pocket, using a contrast coloured sewing thread as follows:
Remove, but do not break, the main yarn from the carriage.
Thread in the cotton then replace the main yarn over the thread.
Hold the thread towards the back of the carriage and knit 1 row.
Remove the thread from the carriage and knit to RC 072.
Bring the empty needles marking the pocket back to WP. Pick up the heels of the adjacent stitches and hang on to the empty needles.
Knit to RC 116(120,124).

Shape V neck:
Dec 1 st at LHS and hang marker thread.
Continue to dec 1 st at neck edge on every following 8th row × 20(20,21) AT THE SAME TIME at RC 160(164,166) shape armholes.
Cast off 10 sts at the beginning of next row. Knit 1 row.
1st and 3rd sizes
Dec 1 st using fully fashioned shaping as on back. (For example, if 5 sts were moved to decrease 2 sts on the back raglan the single decrease here is made by moving only 4 sts therefore dec 1 st.)
Knit 2 rows.
All sizes
Dec 2 sts on next and every following

Opposite: *Raglan style cardigan with picot edge trim for hems, cuffs and band.*

4th row × 25(27,29) RC 268(278,288). Now dec 2 sts on every following alternate row × 2(2,1) RC 270(280,290). Cast off remaining stitch.

Left front

Work as given for right front but reverse the shaping.

Sleeves

(The sleeves are shaped at the top to give a right and left sleeve.)
Cast on with waste yarn over 76(80,84) needles and knit hem as given for back. RC 010. Join hem at MT + I.
Inc I st each end on next and every following 7th row × 26, 128(132,136) sts.
Knit to RC 190(196,200).

Shape armholes:
Cast off 10 stitches at beginning of next 2 rows.
Dec 2 sts each end of very following 4th row × 16(16,15). RC 256(262,262).
Dec 2 sts each end of very following 6th row × 8(9,11).

Shape sleeve top:
1st sleeve: RC 305(317,329) at the end nearest the carriage, cast off 2 sts knit 2 rows.
2nd sleeve: RC 306(318,330) at the end nearest the carriage cast off 2 sts. Knit I row.
Both sleeves: dec I st at neck curve edge on next and following alternate rows X3. AT THE SAME TIME decrease 2 sts at the armhole edge on the 4th row.
Knit the 5 remaining sts with waste yarn for 6–8 rows. Remove from the machine.

Pocket

With the knit side of garment facing, pick up the 40 stitches marked by the sewing thread. Use a single pronged transfer tool and pick up the bar which lies in the centre of the market stitches and hang on to a needle. (See p. 113.)
Pick up the end 'rungs' made by leaving needles in NWP and place on corresponding empty needles.
Knit I row. Pick up next 'rungs', knit across. Continue in this way until all rungs are knitted in and the pocket is complete.

Pocket top

Knit I row MT, 3 rows MT − I, I row MT + I.
Arrange needles to make a picot edge. (Transfer every alternate stitch to an adjacent needle.)
Leave empty needles in WP.
Knit I row MT + I, 3 rows MT − I and I row MT.
Finish with 6–8 rows waste yarn.

Work 2nd pocket in same way.
Slipstitch top of pocket edge into place. Where applicable block and press pieces separately, then join the shoulder seams.

Button and buttonhole bands

These are worked with joins at either the centre back or between the back and sleeve seams, therefore either 2 or 3 sections are made.

The band is worked first, then knitted on to the garment. It is easier to check that the length is correct by knitting the button carrying band first.

To work band over front and sleeve top:
Estimate the number of stitches required – about 166(178,184).
Cast on with waste yarn and knit 6–8 rows.
Knit I row with nylon cord.
MY, I row MT + I, 8 rows MT − I, I row MT + I.
Arrange for picot edge as on pocket top.
Knit I row MT + I, 8 rows MT − I, I row MT + I.

Pick up first row of MY loops between nylon cord to fold band. Knit I row MT + 2.
With purl side of garment facing, pick up front edge and sleeve top, using 3-pronged transfer tool, and place on to needles carrying the band.

Note the number of needles used along straight front edge. These are the stitches over which the buttonholes are worked on the second side band. Knit I row with a large stitch size. Cast off using the latch tool.

Buttonhole band: Work the second side in the same way, but work buttonholes on the 5th and 15th row of the band. 4 buttonholes are worked on this garment. The first and 4th are worked 3 to 4 sts from the marker and waist. Count the remaining needles in work between these buttonholes, then divide that number by 3. This gives the number of needles between the centre of the buttonholes. Once the position of the buttonholes is decided, you can work a buttonhole of your choice. (See p. 113.)

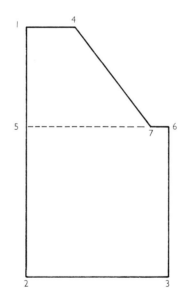

Drawing a raglan block
Add ease to all measurements before drawing. See section on taking measurements (pp. 115–17) before drawing.

1–2   *Back length (B)*
2–3   *Square across from 2, $\frac{1}{4}$ chest measure ($\frac{1}{4}$A)*
1–4   *Square across $\frac{1}{2}$ neck width ($\frac{1}{2}$C)*
1–5   *Armhole depth + raglan ease (E+ raglan ease) square across*
3–6   *Square up from 3 to cut line from 5*
6–7   *$\frac{1}{3}$ cm depending on garment size*
7–4   *Join with diagonal line. Draw neck line as preferred.*

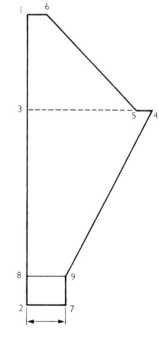

1–2   *Arm + shoulder length (F+$\frac{1}{2}$[D-C])*
1–3   *Armhole depth (E) square across*
3–4   *$\frac{1}{2}$ arm width ($\frac{1}{2}$G)*
4–5   *Length 6–7 on bodice*
1–6   *Square across $\frac{1}{6}$ of neck ($\frac{1}{6}$C) Join 5–6*
2–7   *Square across $\frac{1}{2}$ wrist measure ($\frac{1}{2}$H)*
2–8   *Cuff depth square across*
7–9   *Square up to cut line from 8. Join 9–4.*

A simple buttonhole with a small opening can be made over 2 sts. Transfer the stitches to adjacent needles and knit 1 row with the empty needles left in WP. Two loops are formed over the empty needles, one of these loops must be twisted to make a stitch. Move 1 needle to HP then back so dropping the loop. Take a single-pronged transfer tool and insert it under the dropped loop from back to front. Bring your hand down towards the front of the machine, twisting the stitch loop on the tool. Replace on to the empty needle. Continue knitting.

Back neckband
Work over 51(51,53) needles, using the extra stitches for joining the button and buttonhole bands.

Making up
Sew in sleeves, join side, sleeve and neck borders. Neaten buttonholes and loose ends.

DESIGNING YOUR OWN RAGLAN STYLE JUMPER
The armhole depth is greater for a raglan garment than one with set-in sleeves. Add to armhole depth:

Child	Woman	Man
1.5 cm	2–3 cm	3–4 cm

CARDIGAN DESIGNS
Add to raglan jumper measurements at least 4 cm to the bust/chest and arm width. Deepen the armhole by 1.5–2 cm.

Allowance must be made for the buttonband by taking half the width of the buttonband from the centre front on each side. Sleeve and back length may be slightly larger than the jumper.

PROBLEMS IN PATTERN KNITTING

PROBLEM	CAUSE	REMEDY
Pattern missing	1. Carriage moved forward and back without crossing the knitting	Avoid moving carriage back at the start of a row. If this happens and the card is moved and spotted before you knit, wind the card back to the row required
Pattern missing on electronic machines	1. Pattern not dark enough	Re-draw
	2. Dirty 'eye'	Clean
	3. Sunlight	Shade
Card jamming	1. Card joined incorrectly	Join so that leading edge of card is on the inside of the loop
	2. Torn card	Replace
	3. Card not straight	Straighten
Stitches dropped at the start of the row	1. End stitches not catching 2nd colour	Pull end needles out to HP. Hang claw weights
	2. *Lace:* Stitch transferred to a needle in NWP	*Knitmaster:* Check edge stops in correct place. *Others:* Push selected end needles back to WP
Tucks not knitting properly	1. Tucking over too many rows	Try tucking over fewer rows or a thinner yarn
	2. Too much weight	Remove weights
Weaving yarn not caught under the stitch	1. Weaving brushes worn	Replace
	2. Yarn tension too loose	Tighten tension of yarn
Stitches dropped along row in lace	1. Stitch size too small	Use larger stitch size
	2. Insufficient weight	Add more weight
	3. Machine set at wrong angle	*Toyota:* Knit on flat, not tilted bed
	4. Knitting at wrong angle	Hang lace work over ribber
Fair Isle not knitting properly	1. Stitch size too small	Increase stitch size
	2. 2nd colour yarn wrongly tensioned	adjust tension: *Toyota:* Place 3rd short tension wire on to tension wire holding 2nd colour *Brother:* Slip 2nd colour yarn under lower fine tension wire

CABLES AND FINISHING TOUCHES

CABLES

Cables, or crossed stitches, can be used on any jumper providing a tension swatch is knitted first. They can be worked on all machines. They are made by taking two groups of stitches from the needles, crossing the stitches over, then replacing them on the machine.

MAKING A CABLE

To make a 6 stitch cable, crossing left to right on the knit side of fabric, and using two 3-pronged transfer tools, work as follows:

With one 3-pronged transfer tool take 3 stitches off the machine at RHS of the group of 6 stitches of the cable.
Hold the tool horizontally under the sinker posts.
With the second 3-pronged transfer tool, take the remaining 3 stitches from the group of 6 and transfer them on to the first 3 empty needles.
Bring the first transfer tool up from under the sinker posts and replace the stitches on to the 4th, 5th and 6th empty needles.
Put all 6 needles to HP or UWP.
Knit 6, 8 or 10 rows, then repeat the cable cross again.
Work 6, 8 or 10 rows – the same number each time – between cables. If the LHS stitches are removed first the cable will twist the opposite way.

Combinations of cable transfers can be made to form plaits. 1, 2 or 3 stitches can be crossed in varying combinations, for example, a 4 stitch cable with 2 pairs of stitches crossed, or 1 stitch crossed with 3 stitches.
With chunky yarn cables can only be made over a maximum number of 4 stitches.

TIP

□ *To ease the pull at the crossover of the stitches.*
1. Leave 1 stitch on waste yarn, or a safety pin, at either side of the cabling stitches on the first row of the cable pattern. Place the empty needles in NWP while knitting the pattern. On finishing the cable use the latch tool to

Opposite: A cable sample decorated with cords, pompom, shell edge, woven braid and tassles.

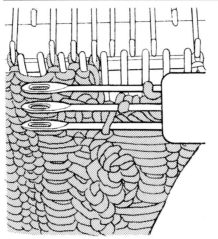

Making a cable:
1. *Hold tool sideways.*

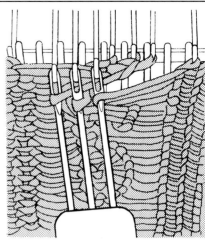

2. *Replace stitches onto empty needles.*

pick up the stitch held at the bottom of the cable, then latch up the ladder at the side of the cable. Repeat with the 2nd stitch on the other side. This reduces the ladder effect and sets the cable in a purl stitch background.
2. If the crossover is still tight, bring the needles in NWP to WP on the row before the cable is worked. Knit this row, then return these needles to NWP, first dropping the loop. The extra length of yarn on this row either side of the cable will allow the stitches to be crossed more easily. The cable is finished by latching up as before.

CORDS AND TRIMS

These extra decorations can be added to your knitting for decoration and an individual touch.

CORDS

These are easily knitted. They can be sewn on to the garment to give a textured effect, or to use as a draw string. (Do not put a cord, or ribbon, round the neck of a baby's garment. This can be fatal.)

Method

Use MT appropriate to yarn thickness.
Cast on 'e'-wrap, or closed edge over 4 needles.
Knit 4 rows. Hold the knitting down or hang claw weights.
Set the carriage to slip in one direction only.
For *Brother, Singer, Toyota:* Set one Part, Slip, or Empty button or lever.
For *Knitmaster:* Set to 'S' with one side lever back the other forward.
For *manual machines:* Cords can be made by putting needles in HP for 1 row, then pushing them back to UWP,

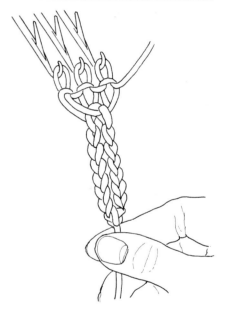

Cord: *hold down firmly to close cord.*

make sure the latches are open, and knitting 1 row.
Repeat these 2 rows.
Knit required length. As you knit, the slipped yarn is pulled across closing the gap to make the cord. To finish put all the stitches on to a bodkin and take the end of the yarn through, pull tight and finish with a stitch to secure the yarn.

SHELL TRIM

This is a lacy effect braid. Many such shell braids can be made. The simplest is a single shell.
Arrange 3 needles in WP I–I–I (– needles in NWP).
Cast on 'e'-wrap.
Knit 4 rows, hold knitting or hang claw weights.

Set carriage to Hold. (see p. 66.)
*Put centre needle to HP. Knit 4–6 rows. (This will depend on the thickness of the yarn.)
Push the needle back to UWP. Knit 2 rows.
Repeat from * for length required. Cast off.

WOVEN BRAID

A flat braid which uses a weaving technique so a thicker yarn can be used.
Needle arrangement 3 needles in WP:
1–1–1 WP
3–2–1 Carriage at RHS
Cast on 'e'-wrap, knit 4 rows.
Take 2nd yarn and hang over needle 1. Knit 1 row.
*The weaving yarn is taken under and over the top of needle 3 in HP. Knit across.
Put needle 1 in HP, take the weaving yarn under and over the needle, knit across.
Repeat from * until the length required is knitted. Cast off. Hold the knitting down as you knit.

POMPOMS AND TASSLES

These can be made using needles pulled out to HP to hold the yarn which is wound round the needles to give a bundle of strands to a required thickness. To make the pompoms on a standard gauge machine put 2 needles in HP about 30 needles apart, and wind the yarn round to give the required thickness. This is then tied with a length of matching yarn in the centre of the bundle. Cut the strands at each needle. Use tieing yarn to attach the pompom.
Tassles are made in a similar way, but with an equal number of strands in each. Once the strands are cut and removed from the machine, fold the bundle in half; attach to fabric using latch tool. Push the latch tool through the fabric and take the folded strands in the hook. Pull hook and tassle through fabric. Now move the tool forward and take the tassle ends in the hook and pull these through the looped strands already on the tool shank.
Remove tool and pull tassle tight.
Repeat for the number needed.

POCKETS

A PATCH POCKET

This is the simplest pocket to knit. A patch of knitting is worked and then sewn in place on the garment. (See jacket pattern pp. 96–100.)

FLAP POCKETS

1. This pocket is made up of two layers attached at the opening and hangs freely inside the garment.

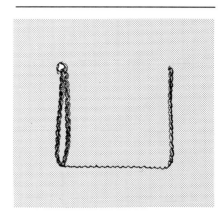

Flap pocket: *inside view.*

2. The flap pocket can also be knitted with a band at the top. The flap is knitted in the same way as style 1, but the added band reduces the stretch of the pocket opening.

Knitting flap pockets

The garment is knitted until the position for the pocket opening is reached. The needles either side of the pocket stitches are then pushed forward to HP, one side at a time. The band is worked first, then over the same stitches knit double the length of knitting required for the depth of the pocket. The needles on either side of the pocket are brought back from HP to WP and the knitting continued to complete the garment. Sew the side edges of the pocket flap together, stitch the row ends of the band in place.

SINGLE THICKNESS POCKET

This pocket has the three edges sewn to the main garment. This can also be knitted with a band. Care is needed when sewing the pocket to prevent the outline showing on the garment front.

A single thickness pocket can be knitted in position after the main garment

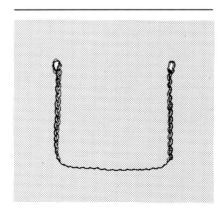

Single thickness pocket: *inside view.*

is knitted, this pocket is knitted on the outside of the garment. (*See raglan pattern pp. 105–108.*)

Knitting single thickness pockets

either:
Knit the pocket lining separately before starting to knit the garment and keep it on waste yarn. When the position for the pocket is reached, either cast off the appropriate stitches or work a band.
The stitches from the pocket lining are then placed on the empty needles and the main knitting completed. The pocket is sewn into place on completion of the garment.
or
The main garment is knitted with the pocket position outlined, the sides with a 'ladder' formed by needles in NWP and the base by a marker thread. On completion of the main garment, the base stitches are picked up and the pocket knitted on to the front of the garment. The sides are attached as the pocket is knitted.

Practice: Pockets

Use 4 ply [DK] yarn. MT 6–8 [2–3].

Method 1: Flap pocket

Work 'e-wrap' cast on over 40 [30] needles.
Knit 30 [18] rows.
Set machine to Hold. At the opposite end to the carriage put 10 [7] needles to HP and knit 1 row.
At the opposite end to the carriage put 10 [7] needles to HP, then over the remaining 20 [16] stitches knit 30 [18] rows MT, 1 row MT − 1, 30 [18] rows MT.
Hang claw weights on pocket edges as required. Return the needles from HP to UWP at the opposite side to the carriage and knit across.
Cancel Hold setting. Re-set RC to 30 [18].
Knit to RC 40 [24]. Do not cast off. Change yarn for one of a different colour if available and continue knitting.

Method 2: Flap pocket with welt top

Knit 30 [18] rows and arrange the needles as in method 1 with 20 [16] needles remaining in WP for pocket. Thread the nylon cord into the carriage WITH the main yarn. Secure the free end. Knit 1 row. Remove the nylon cord from the carriage. Knit 6 [4] rows MT − 1, 1 row MT, 6 [4] rows MT − 1. Pick up the stitches along the bottom line of the nylon cord.
Knit the pocket as in Method 1. Then bring the needles, held at the side, back

to WP and knit 10 [6] more rows. Remove nylon cord. Do not cast off. Change yarn colour.

Method 3: Single thickness pocket knitting on to garment

Knit 10 rows. Transfer the 10th [8th] stitch either side of O on to the 11th [9th] needle. Put the empty needles to NWP.

Take a length of sewing thread in a contrast colour and secure one end. Remove the main yarn from the carriage and put in the thread. Replace the main yarn in front of the thread. Hold the thread to the back of the machine and knit 1 row. The thread will show on the knit side. Remove thread from carriage. Knit 20 [16] rows. Pick up the heel at the base of the 11th [9th] stitch either side of O and place it on the 10th [8th] needle brought back to WP. Knit 10 [6] rows. Cast off.

With the knit side of the sample facing, pick up the loop of the ladder at one side of the pocket position and hook it on to the 10th [8th] needle at RHS or LHS of centre O.

Work along the pocket base, picking up the bar in the stitches marked by the sewing thread (not between the

stitches). Pick up the ladder loop on the second side of the pocket. Knit 1 row. Pick up a ladder loop at each side of the pocket and hook it on to the 10th [8th] needles. Knit 1 row.

Continue working in this manner until all the loops are worked. Work a band by knitting 6 [4] rows MT − 1, 1 row MT − 1, 6 [4] rows MT − 1. Finish with waste yarn and then sew in position.

Method 4: Single thickness pocket knitted first

Pocket lining: Work 'e-wrap' cast on over 20 [16] needles.
Knit 32 [18] rows MT. Finish on waste yarn.
Sample piece: Work 'e-wrap' cast on over 40 [30] needles.
Knit 36 [20] rows MT.
Cast off the centre 20 [16] sts with a separate length of yarn, or set the machine as for Method 1 (flap pocket) and knit a band. Finish on waste yarn. Hook the stitches of the pocket lining, held on waste yarn, on to the empty needles. Remove waste yarn. Return any needles to WP from HP and finish by knitting 10 [6] rows. Cast off.
Sew the pocket flap in place on the purl side (the inside) of the sample.

number of needles over which the buttonholes will be worked as two holes are needed for each side of the buttonhole band.

Methods of making buttonholes

Small buttonholes: Transfer 1 stitch to the adjacent needle and leave the empty needle in WP. Knit across to make the hole.

Larger buttonholes: 2 stitches are transferred on to adjacent needles, one to the LHS and one to the RHS. Leave the empty needles in WP. Knit 1 row. You will see loops of yarn over the buttonhole needles, if the knitting were continued a ladder would form. To avoid this, drop a loop from one of the needles. Take the single pronged transfer tool and put it under the dropped loop, from the back to the front of the machine. Twist the tool, and thus the yarn, by bringing the tool to the front of the machine. Replace the twisted loop on to the empty needle. Continue knitting.

Three or four stitch sewn buttonholes: In the position where the buttonhole is required, use a length of contrast yarn

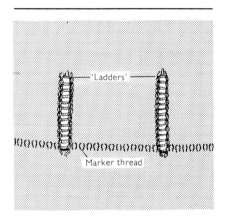

Single thickness pocket: first stage markings on main garment.

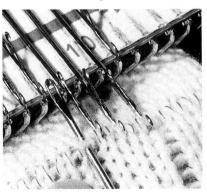

Single thickness pocket: picking up stitches.

BUTTON BANDS AND BUTTONHOLES

BUTTON BANDS

Button bands are worked using the same methods as neckbands. A better finish to the garment is obtained if the band is knitted sideways rather than lengthways on the single bed machine. Bands knitted as a hem on every needle, using the hem tension MT − 2, give a very neat finish. The bands are knitted either directly on to the edge of the front of the cardigan or jacket, or knitted first then attached to the edge.

BUTTONHOLES

The position of the buttonholes are governed by the number of buttons required and the length of the band. To position the buttonholes evenly, estimate the number of stitches over which the band will be worked.

Decide the positions of the first and last buttonholes, remembering that a cardigan buttoning at the neck may have a buttonhole in the neckband. Then, using the numbers on the needle protection strip, count the needles between the first and last buttons and divide this figure by the number of remaining buttons + 1. This gives the number of needles between the centre of each buttonhole. Make a note of the

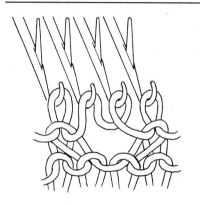

Two-stitch buttonhole, with one stitch twisted.

Three stitch buttonhole knitted in WY.

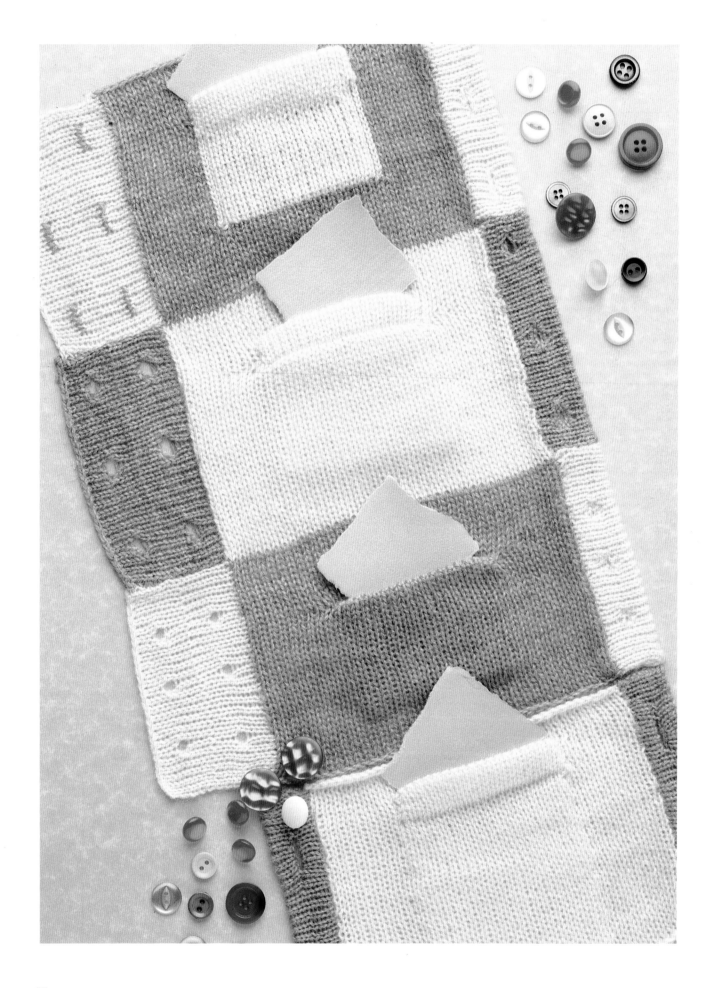

and knit by hand the number of stitches required for the buttonhole. Continue knitting and repeat on the second side of the band. On completion of the band, the contrast yarn is carefully unpicked and the two sides sewn together along the edges of the buttonhole.

Four stitch knitted buttonhole: The first side of the band is worked as in the previous method with 4 stitches knitted in contrast yarn.

Work the second side up to the buttonhole row. Using a single-pronged transfer tool, pick up 5 loops of MY at the top of the contrast yarn knitted on the buttonhole on the first side. Each loop is placed into the hook of the same needle used on the first side, the 5th loop being put on to a needle at the LHS.
Allow the stitches already on the needles to slip behind the latches.
Pull the picked-up loops through the stitches on the needle.
Now cast off these stitches. Start at the RHS of the 5 stitches and transfer the 2nd stitch on to the first needle hook. Pull the 2nd stitch through the first stitch in order to cast it off. Remove the remaining stitch from needle 1 back to needle 2.
Repeat, transferring the 3rd stitch to needle 2 and casting off stitch 2.
Continue until 4 buttonhole stitches have been cast off.
Using the single-pronged transfer tool, pick up 4 loops from the 2nd edge of the contrast yarn, remembering to pick up MY, and hook these loops on to the empty needles.
If 2 extra loops either side of the buttonhole are picked up then the pull of the cast-off stitches is reduced.
Finish the band. The waste yarn is unpicked to open the buttonholes.

TIP
□ *Try knitting the buttonhole row on the 2nd side, where the cast-off edge is made, on a larger stitch size. The looser row may not be noticeable and the casting off process is easier.*

Opposite: *Small-scale samples illustrating pockets. (From top) Method 3, p. 113 – single thickness pocket knitted on to garment with 3 stitch buttonholes (LHS buttonholes after knitting and before sewing, RHS finished buttonholes); Method 2, p. 112 – flap pocket with welt top and 2 stitch buttonholes (LHS knitted; RHS finished); Method 1, p. 112 – simple flap pocket with single stitch buttonholes (LHS knitted, RHS finished); Method 4, p. 113 – single thickness pocket with 4 stitch machine knitted buttonholes.*

Four Stitch Buttonholes

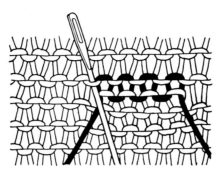

Pick up 5 loops at top of contrast yarn

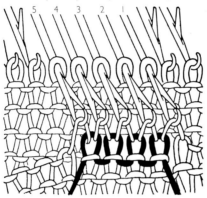

Place loops in same needles used in knitting waste yarn and 1 extra at LHS. Pull through stitches on needle.

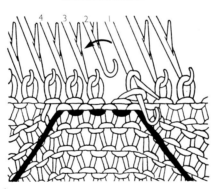

Cast off stitches: *Transfer 2nd st. onto 1st needle. Cast off by pulling 2nd st. through 1st needle st. Transfer 2nd st. back to 2nd needle. Continue until 4 st. cast off.*

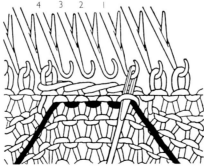

Pick up 4 loops from 2nd edge of contrast yarn. Finish band.

TAKING MEASUREMENTS

Wherever possible TAKE THE ACTUAL BODY MEASUREMENTS of the person you are knitting for. See p. 116. The table on p. 117 which is offered as a guide for those who wish to work out their own pattern, but are unable to take the appropriate measurements. It is based on a classic set-in sleeve jumper for a 'standard' body.

WHERE TO TAKE MEASUREMENTS
Chest/bust: Round the fullest part gives 'size' as quoted in patterns.
An extra amount must be added to this measurement to allow for 'ease' of movement.
Centre back to waist: From the bone at the back of the neck to the natural waist line. Extra length is added to suit the style and the wearer's requirements.
Back width: Measured across the back at shoulder level.
Arm length: Taken from the shoulder to the wrist.
Upper arm: This measurement is taken round the fullest part of the upper arm. Again ease is added to allow for movement.
Wrist: Measured round a clenched fist.
Shoulder: Measured from the base of the neck to the shoulder point.
Armhole depth: The measurement is taken from the shoulder point, round under the arm and back to the shoulder point. This length is then halved and ease added. Armhole depth measurements vary greatly on patterns depending on current fashion and the wearer's preference.
Back neck: Measured across the back of the base of the neck. This is sometimes taken as one third of the back width measurement.

EASE
The following tables are a guide to the amounts to be added to a body measurement. They are all given in centimetres.

	Adult	Child
Chest/Bust	5–10 cm	3–5 cm
Armhole depth	2.5–4 cm	1.5–2.5 cm
Upper arm	5–12.5 cm	4–8 cm

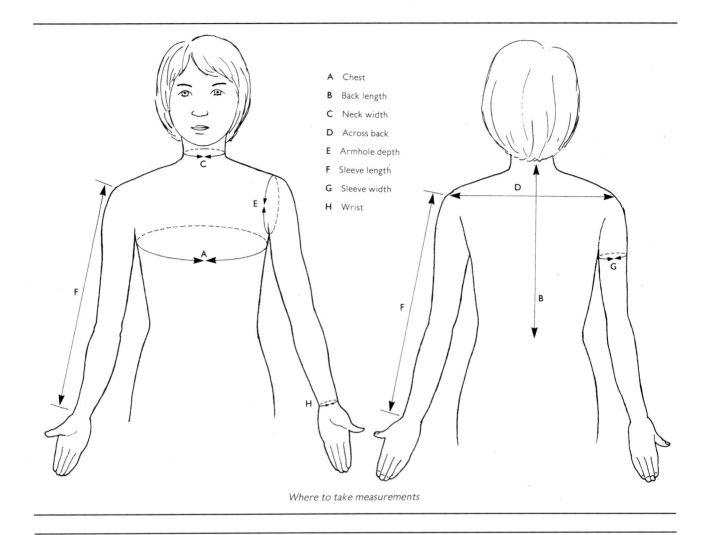

A Chest

B Back length

C Neck width

D Across back

E Armhole depth

F Sleeve length

G Sleeve width

H Wrist

Where to take measurements

Set-in-sleeve: Front/back bodice with ease added

1–2 Centre back length (B)
Square across from 1 and 2
1–3 $\frac{1}{2}$ neck width ($\frac{1}{2}$C)
1–4 Armhole depth + shoulder slope (E + shoulder slope)
4–5 Square across $\frac{1}{4}$ chest measure, ($\frac{1}{4}$A)
6 Square down from 5 to cut line from 2
4–7 $\frac{1}{2}$ cross back width ($\frac{1}{2}$D)
8 Square up from 7 to cut line from 1.
Draw dotted line.
8–9 Shoulder slope depth. Join 3–9.
5–10 1–3 cm depending on garment size
Draw curve from 10 to line from 7–9.
Draw chosen neck line, round or 'V'.

Set-in-sleeve: The sleeve with ease added

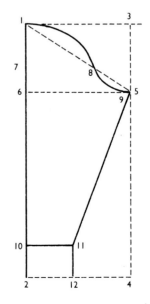

1–2 Sleeve length (F)
Square across from 1 and 2
3+4 Mark on lines from 1 and 2 $\frac{1}{2}$ sleeve width ($\frac{1}{2}$G)
Join 3–4 with dotted line
1–5 From 1 draw dotted line armhole depth (E) to cut line 3–4
5–6 Square across from 5. Mark 6 on line 1–2.
1–7 $\frac{2}{3}$ length 1–6.
7–8 Square across to cut line 1–5 mark
8 Curve change point
5–9 Length 5–10 on bodice. Draw sleeve head curve from 9–1 through 8. Length of sleeve head seam is the same as the bodice armhole depth (1 or 2 cm longer is acceptable).
2–10 Cuff depth. Square cross $\frac{1}{2}$ cuff width 10–11 (H)
11–12 Square down to line 2–4. Join 11–5.

MEASUREMENTS FOR SET-IN-SLEEVE STYLE JUMPER FOR 'STANDARD' BODY

		18	20	22	24	26	28	30	32	34	36	38	40	42	44	46	
Actual chest/bust in inches		18	20	22	24	26	28	30	32	34	36	38	40	42	44	46	
Actual chest/bust in cm		45	50	55	60	65	70	75	80	85	90	95	100	105	110	115	

KNITTED MEASUREMENTS IN CENTIMETRES (ease and extra length included)

Measurement		18	20	22	24	26	28	30	32	34	36	38	40	42	44	46	
Chest/Bust		50	55	60	66	70	76	82	88	96	101	107	112	117	122	127	**A**
Back length	*child*	33	35	37	42	44	48	51									**B**
	woman								55	56	57	61	62	64	65		
	man										63	65	66	67	69	70	
Neck width	*child+ woman*	12	12	13	13	13.5	14	14	14.5	14.5	15	15.5	16	16.5	18	19.5	**C**
	man								15	15.5	16	17	18	19.5	20	21	
Across back (between armholes)	*child*	20	23	26	28	30	32	33	34								**D**
	woman							34	36	38	40.5	43	44	46.5	49	50.5	
	man										44	46	48	48.5	49	51.5	
Armhole depth	*child*	12.5	13	14	14.5	15	16	18	20								**E**
	woman								22	23	24	25	26	27	28	28	
	man										25	26	27	28	29	29	
Sleeve length	*child*	27	31	36	39	42	44	46	48								**F**
	woman								52	54	56	58	59	59.5	60	60	
	man									58	59	60	61	62	62.5	63	
Sleeve width	*child*	22	23	24	25	27	28	30	32								**G**
	woman							33	35	37	38	39	40	40.5	41	42	
	man									38	39	40	41	42	43	43	
Wrist		14.5	15	15.5	16	16.5	17	18	20	20.5	21	22	22.5	23	24	24.5	**H**

NOTE: *Remember to add ease when using your own measurements*

USING CHARTING DEVICE

1. Draw your garment shapes on to the sheets provided, full scale for the Knitleader (Brother), Knit Tracer (Toyota) and Knit Copy (Singer), or either half or full scale drawings for the Knit Radar (Knitmaster), depending on the model. For garment pieces which are symmetrically shaped, only half of the pieces need be drawn.

2. Knit a tension swatch using the stitches and yarns which are going to be used in the garment.

3. Measure the swatch using a tape measure or the Knitmaster green or blue ruler.

4. Select the appropriate stitch scale and set the rows on the rotating section of the device.

5. To check the shaping try a dry run.

TIP

☐ *If you need to dec/inc several stitches at once it is only possible to cast off/on at the same end of the row as the carriage. If the carriage is at the opposite end, then knit one more row, so moving the chart again; if this means more stitches are now needed to be dec/inc, it is quite acceptable to cast off or on all in one go, so dec/inc the total number of stitches required for the two rows.*

EXTRA MEASUREMENTS FOR PATTERN DRAWING

	Infants	Children	Women	Men
Shoulder slope (drop from base of neck to shoulder point)	1 cm	2 cm	2.5–3 cm	3–4 cm
Back neck shaping (depth of neck)		1 cm	2 cm	3 cm
Front neck shaping (depth) (See also p. 80.)	2.5 cm	5 cm	7.5 cm	10 cm

Lacy top (stitch pattern p. 59) and round neck jumper (stitch pattern p. 84) with set-in sleeves, both knitted in acrylic.

USEFUL ODDS AND ENDS

MACHINE CARE AND MAINTENANCE

GENERAL

1. Keep the machine covered when not in use.
2. Plastic machine covers can be purchased or you can make your own.
3. Electronic machines should be kept out of direct sunlight. Do not leave the machine switched on when not in use. If you have to leave the machine half way through a garment, switch off leaving the programme in the machine. When you switch on again the programme will continue normally.
4. Brush the hairs and fluff from your machine at least after each garment, preferably more often. Brush both the needle bed and under the carriage. On electronic Brother machines remember to keep the 'eye' at the back of the carriage clean. Brush the fluff out of the socket and connector on the Knitmaster Electronic.
5. Oil your machine regularly. Refer to the instruction book to find where oil should be applied. A build-up of used or dried oil can be removed by using white spirit on a soft cloth or paper kitchen towel. Then re-oil. The silicone spray may mistakenly be suggested as a substitute for oil but it is for use on yarn, *not* on the machine.
6. Check that the brushes under the sinker plate assembly run smoothly. (See sinker plate assembly p. 23.)

REPLACEMENT OF NEEDLES

Most modern machines have a needle retaining bar located at the front of the machine, under the front edge of the needle bed.
To replace a needle: Remove this needle retaining bar by first pushing it with a screwdriver or thin pencil at one end, then pulling the other end out from under the needle bed.
Remove the needle by pushing its butt forwards; the shank end should then spring up between the slots on the needle bed.
Close the latch over the hook; then take the shank end and pull the needle backwards until it is clear of the machine.

Insert the new needle using the reverse procedure.
Put the hook end into the slot in the needle bed; move it forward until the shank end is over the slot; then press down on the needle butt and move the needle back until it reaches NWP.
Use the straight end of the needle pusher to hold the hook ends of the needles down on to the needle protection strip and push the needle retaining bar back into place.

OPTIONAL EXTRAS

COLOUR CHANGER

An extra yarn tension arm, sinker plate assembly and a yarn holder for up to 4 colours enable the different coloured yarns to be changed easily and quickly when knitting. The colour changer is used when knitting stripes, 2-colour tuck and slip stitch patterns, or changing the 2nd colour in Fair Isle patterns.

GARTER BAR

This is a metal, comb-like bar used to turn stitches. The stitches are pulled on to the bar and the fabric held on the bar while it is turned. The fabric lies on top of the bar and then the stitches are caught back on to the needles and the bar removed. The garter bar is used to make a fabric with rows of plain (all knit) stitches or to weave added yarns vertically.

GARTER CARRIAGE

This is a motorised carriage made by Brother which automatically knits plain and purl stitches along a row. When used with a punchcard or an electronic pattern programme it forms patterns of knit and purl stitches. As it is motorised it runs independently, stopping at a pre-programmed point or if the yarn breaks. This carriage is available for one make only (Brother).

INTARSIA CARRIAGE

This is used when knitting intarsia, or picture knitting, with 2 or more colours in a row. Each colour is knitted separately and there are no floats. The carriage enables this method of pattern knitting to be used, although some machines have a built-in intarsia facility, so check this before buying the carriage.

LINKER FOR CASTING OFF

This is an additional carriage which casts off stitches using a similar method to that where the latch tool is used. It provides a quick way of casting off.

LINKER FOR SEWING

This is a machine designed to chain stitch knitted fabrics together. The two layers of fabric are held on prongs on a circular bed and a needle sews them together.

SEVEN-PRONGED ADJUSTABLE TRANSFER TOOL

This consists of 7 adjustable prongs in a handle. The prongs can be arranged as required, for example, to transfer every other stitch in a picot edge.

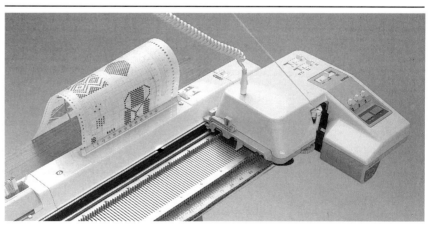

The Brother garter carriage automatically knits patterns of knit and purl stitches in the same row.

ADDRESSES

MACHINE MANUFACTURERS

Jones & Brother,
Shepley Street,
Guide Bridge,
Audenshaw,
Manchester
M34 5JD

Knitmaster,
39–45 Cowleaze Road,
Kingston-on-Thames,
Surrey
KT2 6DT.

Singer,
S.D.L. Ltd.,
Grafton Way,
West Ham Industrial Estate,
Basingstoke,
Hampshire
RG22 6HZ.

Toyota,
Aisin (UK) Ltd.,
Toyota Sewing & Knitting,
34 High Street,
Bromley,
Kent.

POSTAL MACHINE KNITTING CLUB

To & Fro,
Metropolitan Sewing Machines,
321 Ashley Road,
Parkstone,
Poole
BH14 0AP.

YARN MANUFACTURERS

For your information here is a list of the manufacturers of the yarns used in this book:

Amberyarn,
Greendale Mills,
Windhill,
Shipley,
West Yorkshire
BD18 1QB

Argyll Wools Ltd.,
PO Box 15,
Priestley Mills,
Pudsey,
West Yorkshire,
LS28 9LT.

Atkinson Yarn Designer Collection,
Terry Mills,
Ossett,
West Yorkshire
WF5 9SA.

F.W. Bramwell & Co. Ltd.,
Unit 5,
Metcalf Drive,
Altham Lane,
Altham,
Accrington
BB5 5TU

Bonnie's Wools,
164 Bridge Street West,
Newtown,
Birmingham
B19 2YX.

T. Forsell & Son Ltd.,
Blaby Road,
South Wigston,
Leicester
LE8 2SG

The Wool House,
105 High Road,
Chiswick,
London W4.

INDEX

NB: Page numbers in *italics* refer to illustrations.

ACKNOWLEDGEMENTS

AUTHOR'S ACKNOWLEDGEMENTS

I am grateful to Mr Dennis at Tyson's Sewing & Knitting Machine Centre, 40 High Street, Hounslow, Middlesex for the loan of knitting machines during photography.
Thanks to Sue and Steve Newell for help with typing, students Gwen and Beryl for help in knitting the puppets, and my family for going without sweaters while I was writing this book.

ILLUSTRATION ACKNOWLEDGEMENTS

The publishers are grateful to the following for the loan of material during photography:

Knitting machines: Tyson's Sewing & Knitting Machine Centre, Hounslow
Clothes: Marks and Spencers, Baker Street, London
Scarves: Cornelia James, New Bond Street, London
Jewellery: Accessorize, Carnaby Street, London
The Irish Shop, Duke Street, London
Hair and make-up: Gena Dry
Stylist (model shots): Liz Artindale
Stylist (flat shots): Kit Johnson

The Photographs

The Hamlyn Publishing Group/Michael Dent: pp. 44, 62, 64 (both), 69, 96, 113.
The Hamlyn Publishing Group/David Johnson: back cover, 10–11, 12, 14–15, 16, 18–19, 20, 22, 23, 34–5, 38–9, 42, 45, 46–7, 48, 54, 59, 67, 70, 74, 75, 78–9, 82–3, 86, 90, 91, 94, 98, 99, 102, 103, 107, 110, 114 120.
The Hamlyn Publishing Group/Fiona Pragoff: front cover, frontispiece, 26–7, 30–31, 37, 50–51, 63, 118–19.
Knitmaster: pp. 80.
All line illustrations: The Hamlyn Publishing Group/Peter Bull, Gillingham
Colour illustrations: The Hamlyn Publishing Group/Jacqueline Bissett, London